GARDENING WITH FOLIAGE PLANTS

Leaf Bark and Berry

GARDENING WITH FOLIAGE PLANTS

Leaf
Bark
and
Berry

ETHNE CLARKE

With Photographs by CLIVE NICHOLS

ABBEVILLE PRESS · PUBLISHERS · NEW YORK · LONDON · PARIS

First published in the United States of America in 1997 by
Abbeville Press, 488 Madison Avenue, New York, N.Y. 10022

First published in Great Britain in 1996 by
David & Charles, Brunel House, Newton Abbot, TQ12 4PU, England

First edition
2 4 6 8 10 9 7 5 3 1

Art Editor Michael Whitehead
Illustrations Diana Leadbetter

ISBN 0-7892-0330-8

CONTENTS

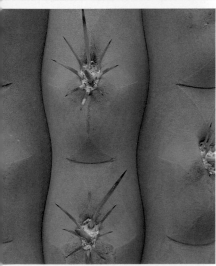

FOREWORD

FOLIAGE WAS NOT MY FIRST INTEREST WHEN I BEGAN gardening, I must admit. Flower color was all and everything to me. I spent hours plotting Jekyllian schemes that rarely made the transition from drawing pad to garden border, mostly because I would rather acquire one special plant than a dozen of a certain color. I soon got tired of shouldering the responsibility of trying to orchestrate year-round color though—something was always out of tune.

It was the Stream Garden at Hidcote in England that opened my eyes. It is the lowest point in the topography of that splendid garden and the water in the little rivulet is completely obscured by an enormous range of equally enormous leaves. The contrasts of forms, leaf shapes, and textures in this group of moisture-loving plants held my attention as no flower border had ever done. The backdrop was formed from the tight clipped hedges that characterize the garden layout at Hidcote, and the whole composition was suddenly revealed to me in layers of various shades of green, from cool silver to dark purples, browns, and reds.

Foliage is the canvas upon which we paint our garden pictures. Green is the perfect foil for flower color and the complex contrasts of form, shape, and texture ease our gardens into the natural landscape.

Beth Chatto's Gold Medal-winning displays at London's Chelsea Flower Show in 1987 were another turning point. Chatto suits the plant to the site rather than trying to adjust the site to accommodate the plant, and she advocates immaculate preparation of the soil. Her compositions are as carefully thought out as any painter's two-dimensional work, achieving an entirely natural effect. This is best studied in her garden at Elmstead Market in Essex, England, and I soon beat a path to her gate determined to apply her techniques to my newly-acquired empty field in central Norfolk, England. If you can't visit the Chatto garden, then I highly recommend her book, *The Green Tapestry*.

Pippa Rakusen, too, and her treasure-filled garden Lyng Beeches near Leeds, England, taught me much about the beauty of woodland gardening; she was as generous with her knowledge as with cuttings, plants, and seed, convinced that I would learn from her and give the plants a good home. Her book *Foliage and Form Throughout the Year* was my first primer on the subject, and copies can be obtained by mail from the Northern Horticultural Society at Harlow Carr, Harrogate, England; the gardens are also worth a visit.

A visit to East Central Texas took me to Peckerwood Gardens where John Fairey relies on the blue-gray shades of fleshy-leaved succulents and sculptural agaves to visually cool the view of the garden from the house. Dusk fell before he and Carl Schoenfeld had shown me the whole garden collection and the neighboring Yucca Do nursery, so we finished by moonlight under which the exotic plants took on an additional layer of glamour as they were reduced entirely to form and texture.

It was while working with Clive Nichols on my book about herb garden design that he and I decided to do a book that would present our enthusiasm for the brilliant design potential of leaves, bark, and berries. We have both spent many years looking at plants and gardens, and increasingly it was the way that foliage was used as the backbone of the garden that caused us the most excitement. We have tried to include as many of the fine leaved plants as we have enjoyed in our journeys through many different types of gardens. Whether driven by the "eco-habitat" gardens at the cutting edge of modern design or the more traditionally inspired formal gardens, all the gardeners mentioned in this book share an interest in growing foliage plants well in the situations that will suit them best. We are indebted to them for sharing their knowledge and gardens with us.

Nevertheless, I am sure many of your favorite foliage plants may be missing, or that some of my favorites wouldn't be looked at twice by someone else. Thankfully, the world — particularly the garden world — is full of different opinions, which is what makes gardening a lively topic of discussion and garden-visiting a major recreational sport. I hope you will take pleasure in the beautiful gardens and plant groupings shown here and find as much inspiration in them as I have. I hope, too, that we will succeed in firing your passion for leaf, bark, and berry.

Ethne Clarke

Yaxham, Norfolk, England

March 1996

IN A GREEN GARDEN

*"Our country is one complete garden, each
section adding its chorus to the great symphony."*
Siftings, *Jens Jensen, 1939.*

FOR CENTURIES WE HAVE BEEN CREATING GARDENS, TRYING to "improve on nature" and exercise control over our environment. Gardeners have manipulated the lines of the natural terrain, altered the course of rivers, or introduced water where it did not naturally exist. They have even gone so far as to create artificial environments — rockeries, peat gardens, bog gardens, and the like — to nurture a garden full of colorful exotics. We are steeped in that tradition and have added to it our own lavish use of hard-landscaping features: stone walls, sweeping terraces, paved paths, electric fountains and waterfalls, and artificial lighting. Much of the display is intended to give structure to the garden and to retain interest after the flowers have faded.

However, there is another way for the garden to hold our attention throughout the year, a way to work with nature that allows for the development of a more relaxed and natural style of planting, and one that is more harmonious with our surroundings. There is no easier way to understand this approach than to step beyond your own garden. Take

A formal garden of evergreen topiary frames the natural landscape of meadows and tree-lined streams which inspired the landscape architect Capability Brown to reject the artifice of formality and "improve on nature" in his designs.

The landscape appears in layers of foliage: tree canopy, understory plantings of shrubs, perennials, annuals, and groundcovers. These are also the basics of garden design against which flower and berry color comes and goes.

a good hard look at the natural landscape around you and the meaning of Jensen's words will become immediately apparent. If we regard the plants in our gardens as notes of music and ourselves as musicians, we should be studying how nature composes her symphonies and then trying to adapt her variations and repetitions of foliage colors, textures, forms, and shapes to formulate the theme of our own garden.

Foliage is displayed in the natural landscape in layers, and each layer imposes its own conditions on the environment. The primary layer is the tree canopy; beneath this layer are the shrubs and, lower still, the perennials and what I term "ephemerals," the annual and biennial tribe. At the bottom are the groundcovers, which include plants from the shrub and the perennial groups. These layers interact, creating a variety of growing conditions, such as the deep shade cast by a group of densely leaved trees, or damp soil conserved by the use of groundcovering plants. Follow nature and you are on the way to creating a garden where the harmonies of the seasons are captured in the repeated theme of beautiful leaves accented by the passing show of flowers and berries.

Shelters, backgrounds, and screens

Shelters

Trees have the most immediate and obvious influence on our landscape because of their height and longevity, and the ways in which they are used give the landscape its shape in large part. First and foremost, trees are used to provide shelter belts and each region will have its own requirements, determined by climate. A windy coastal garden will benefit from a mixed screen of evergreens and deciduous trees to mitigate the effect of salt-laden breezes and to cut wind speeds through the garden. An inland garden in a mild temperate zone would benefit sufficiently from a single row of deciduous trees whose trunks and branches would provide all the necessary wind shield.

The key to the success of a shelter belt relies less on which trees are used (although you should aim to use species that appear naturally in your area) than on the provision of a uniformly dense screen according to the degree of protection required. This can be either a wide plantation belt of evergreens, or a more open boundary of mixed deciduous trees which will

Deciduous trees like this *Aesculus × carnea* make a statement all year-round, from the moment the fresh green leaf buds burst to the moment they drop to spread a golden carpet on the ground.

allow light to filter through and create the sensation of a woodland edge. Such a scheme could then be planted with shrubs and herbaceous perennials that would benefit from the low light and moist conditions such a tree planting would offer. Also, bear in mind that it is only necessary for a shelter belt to contain two or three species, which should be planted in clusters rather than uniform lines. Again, the best teacher is nature, so look around carefully.

When planning a shelter belt, there are various things you should consider. First, the seasonal wind directions. In my garden in Norfolk, England, the prevailing winds are from southwest to northeast during spring and summer, then sweeping around to northwest to southeast in the autumn and winter. This is not unlike the wind patterns of the prairies of the American Midwest which, curiously, Norfolk resembles in other ways, including the big blue skies and large fields (relatively speaking). Knowing this, I planted trees to shelter the garden from the worst of winter's Siberian winds and to filter the strong gusts that blow in during early spring. The shelter belt will in time be tall enough to carry the wind over its top so that wind continues to move some distance across the garden before it touches ground again. The filtered effect of the less densely planted windbreak slows the summer breeze as it moves through the garden, so that, hopefully, the delphiniums won't be flattened and the mood of the garden will be enhanced by soft breezes.

In small urban gardens, trees are used as wind shields simply because a true shelter belt would take up too much space. A few trees planted in a loose group in the direction of the prevailing wind will suffice to slow the breeze. Good air circulation is important for healthy plant growth, and this is especially important in the close environment of a town garden. Urban gardens are often fenced or walled, and these permanent structures alone do not provide a garden-friendly service since the wind will rise over the top and fall straight down the other side, creating a potentially damaging eddy. A few trees planted several feet away from the wall will, however, break the eddy and soften the blow of the wind as it falls on the plants below.

Shelters do provide an ornamental background, but since their primary purpose is functional you will naturally adopt a different set of selection and planting criteria from those you would use when making a purely aesthetic choice.

Trees are also able to modify the climate within a garden. Apart from providing shade and shelter, they also help to keep ambient moisture levels up because the leafy canopy retards evaporation of water from the soil and also releases water into the atmosphere through transpiration (one of the processes of photosynthesis), one of the reasons why the decimation of the tropical rainforests threatens the survival of our species. On a more parochial level, leaf canopies cut airborne dust particles, keep the soil cool, and by exchanging oxygen and carbon dioxide, increase air purity in the garden environs.

Backgrounds

Background plants should relate to the foreground plants, so if you are planning a low-key shrubbery, don't plant a collection of trees that have strong individual characters; it is better to stick to subtle subjects in harmony with their surroundings. In my garden, which is made from a farm field, most of the plants in the remains of the old hedges have grown into mature trees, so the naturally occurring background is composed of hazelnuts, hollies, crab apples, hawthorn, and field maple (*Acer campestre*). Consequently, the trees I have introduced include apples, more hazels, Italian alder, mulberry, quince, and a small grove of *Prunus* "Tai-Haku," the great white cherry, for a spectacular spring display of pink new leaves framing the clusters of white flowers, and an autumn show of reds and orange. My biggest mistake was a single poplar which looks as if it has grown taller than the garden is long and brings me to the next point.

Backgrounds can also serve as frames for a distant view, allowing you to borrow the landscape. This was a favorite trick of architects in Renaissance Italy, who adhered to the dictate proposed by Alberti in *On the Art of Building in Ten Books*, that a beautiful vista framed by the garden should be incorporated in every landscape design. But just as a painting and its frame must be sympathetic, so a garden frame should relate to the landscape by repeating the dominant forms in that view; a vista of rugged mountain peaks should be set off by strong verticals and conical shapes, with low mounds in the foreground to replicate the appearance of the landscape forms. Low, rolling hills and soft curves forming the view would find a sympathetic frame in a composition of rounded tree and shrub shapes, with clump-forming foliage perennials repeating the forms in the foreground. It is not enough, however, simply to repeat the forms in the view — you must also keep them in proportion, which is why I should never have planted that poplar. It is a strident vertical completely out of scale with the size of the garden and the rounded forms of the old hedgerow trees and the other trees that have been planted.

The silvery nimbus of *Pyrus salicifolia* gives a soft focus background to the clearly defined geometry of a clipped box knot garden and the metal-frame arbor clothed in evergreen ivy *Hedera* "Parsley Crested."

Tonal contrasts give a garden vitality; the play of pale against dark, shadow against light can be achieved by using bright leaved plants to enhance the shadowy areas of garden, effectively adding visual depth to the layout.

Screening

Trees are also often used to provide screening, either to create seclusion within the garden or else to prevent the intrusion of unsightly elements from outside the garden boundaries. In a small garden, a screen will be linear, such as a row of evergreens or a line of pleached trees (usually beech or hornbeam), or will be a single specimen planted to block out an individual eyesore like a telephone pole. In a rural garden, there will be more room to plant small groups of trees, or even thickets of one species. Start to do this, and you will be following in the footsteps of Capability Brown; if he couldn't demolish an offending element in the landscape such as a group of farm-worker's cottages, he transplanted entire woodlands to obliterate it. Whatever the case, strive to keep the proportions and shapes in harmony with the background and surroundings.

Shade is the other important contribution made by trees to the garden, and it provides more than just a place to sit out of the sun. The effect of contrasts in garden design can never be overstated, and the visual impact of light shade, deep shade, and dappled shade can draw you through a garden as surely as a path of expensive stone paving.

The amount of shade you require will depend on the quantity of sun your garden receives and how you use your garden (including what you want to grow). During hot summer months the sun is high in the sky, almost directly overhead; during winter it moves across the sky at a lower angle. You may need the most shade from the middle part of the day to the evening on a terrace used for barbecues and evening meals, or you may require day-long shade over a specific part of the garden to protect moisture-loving plants.

The uniform pattern of four box-hedged squares provides a well-defined contrast to the informality of the surrounding planting scheme

Selecting trees to provide shade requires you to consider their structure; whether they have large leaves, densely crowded branches, and heavy crowns, or whether the leaves are small and loosely fill the fine branches on light, open crowns. The denser the shade the more cooling effect will be felt by people beneath the trees, but the less easy it will become to grow a wide range of plants below.

Shade is an important consideration when planting evergreens; the dense shade they create will be permanent and so could have an adverse effect if, for instance, it is necessary to allow some warming sunlight to filter through to a group of plants during winter, or even to allow the weak but cheering rays of the winter sun to brighten a living room. To be perpetually subject to gloomy shadows is enervating, so it would be best to choose among the deciduous trees.

Hedges

Many trees are used to form hedges; this is their most potent structural use in landscaping. A formal hedge is usually a repeated planting of one single variety of tree, regularly pruned to encourage branching along the entire length of the trunk to create a dense barrier.

Most people prefer evergreen hedges, but too often they miss the opportunity to do something that will be of long-term benefit to the landscape and plant the ubiquitous Lawson cypress (x *Cupressus lawsoniana*) instead of the far superior yew (*Taxus baccata*) out of the misguided belief that yew is too slow-growing. Actually, the reverse is true, and the Lawson cypress is too fast-growing. A well-planted yew hedge, fed regularly with high nitrogen in early spring and general balanced fertilizer in the summer and watered regularly until established, will easily make 12-18 in. (30-45 cm) growth in a year. A cypress will do more, of course, but is extremely vigorous, and could require two or three clippings each year to keep it in check. Who wants to spend all their time hedge-trimming?

Yew makes the finest ornamental evergreen hedge. Other popular evergreens are holly (golden-variegated holly hedges are quite spectacular), Portuguese laurel (*Prunus lusitanica*), and the larger-leafed *P. laurocerasus*; the last two make a rather gloomy contribution, in spite of their glossy, light-reflective leaves.

Hedges can also be planted with deciduous trees, although the ever-popular beech (*Fagus sylvatica*) behaves like an evergreen, holding its caramel-brown withered leaves until the new foliage appears in the spring. Hornbeam (*Carpinus betulus*) is also widely used, and both trees are excellent when a high yet narrow hedge is required.

Tapestry hedges are a particularly attractive way to create informal or formal boundaries, and are planted using a mix of deciduous and evergreen trees; the old hedge bordering my garden is in effect a tapestry hedge, and against it the loose and extremely informal style of planting in the garden looks completely at ease.

Hedges can serve as screens, wind shields, shelter belts or walls, dividing the garden into separate areas which can then be given individual treatments. Low-growing shrubby plants like dwarf box (*Buxus suffruticosa*), common thyme (*Thymus vulgaris*), certain small-leaf hollies, and similar evergreens are used to make ground-covering linear patterns of tightly clipped hedging. Knot gardens are the most familiar device for taking advantage of these plants, but they can also be used to create ribbons of hedging like a green river to create movement through the landscape.

Hedge preparation and planting

Formal hedges are regularly clipped to maintain a uniform shape, while informal hedges where fruit and flowers are the

Frosted over or even covered in a blanket of snow, the woody structure of the shrubs remains visible throughout winter for true "year-round interest."

main attributes are not clipped other than to preserve an attractive shape. When planting a hedge, remember that while the plants need to be close together to form a dense barrier, their natural growth is as tall-growing trees. While regular pruning and clipping perverts their innate tendency to develop large crowns, it does not disrupt their development of large root systems. If plants are put too closely together they will compete for food and water and some will inevitably die. There is no hard rule about spacing since it will depend on the tree you use, but 2-3 ft. (60-90 cm) is not too much for a yew or hornbeam hedge. Hedging plants can be bought as containered plants or else bare-root in bundles; deciduous hedging can be planted at any time of year, as can evergreens that are in containers, weather permitting (avoid periods of heavy frost or rain). Bare-root evergreens should be planted in the winter or early spring, as they are prone to desiccation and there is more moisture in the air at those times of year. Newly planted evergreens can be sprayed with an anti-desiccant to further assist their establishment. It is best to use young small plants rather than older and hence larger plants, since the youngsters will settle in more quickly and a young hedge if regularly fed will soon catch up in growth. However, if cost is not a factor but instant effects are, and you plan on using older plants, you should also plan to keep them well watered throughout their first year. Prepare a trench at least 3 ft. (90 cm) wide for large hedges, or 18 in. (45 cm) wide for small and dwarf hedges. Double dig the trench, adding plenty of well-rotted manure or soil mix in the bottom layer and slow-release granular fertilizer in the backfill.

The most important thing is to keep a newly planted hedge free of weeds; this can be achieved by routine weeding, forking out perennial weeds, and removing annual weeds before they seed; by spraying with contact and systemic weedkillers; or by mulching. The latter is the most effective measure, and a layer of black plastic spread over the trench and buried along both edges to anchor it will not only keep weeds out, but will help to keep moisture in. The hedging can now be planted through slits

The view through a garden can be enhanced and given a feeling of greater depth by staggering the heights and textures of the hedges, as here where beech hedges alternate with a lime (linden) tree allée.

made in the plastic.

The first or formative pruning techniques vary according to the type of hedging used.

Deciduous, upright-growing plants must be encouraged to establish a framework of branches at, or near to, ground level. In the first year, cut top growth back to within 6 in. (15 cm) of ground level. This removes the leader (main growing stem) and encourages many small branches to develop near the base of the plant. It also ensures that there is not too much top growth

A stilt hedge is a popular visual device for enhancing perspective; here it effectively draws the eye through the garden to the stone arch and finally the countryside beyond. The trees are pollarded to create the effect.

for the underdeveloped root system to support at the same time as the roots are striving to settle into the new site. In the spring of the year following planting, begin shaping the side growth by cutting back some of the new growth.

If, however, the hedge is destined to be a tall-growing wind shield the plants may be left unpruned until established, and then cut back to begin shaping by removing one-third of all the side growth.

Evergreens such as Lawson cypress should be staked in the first year with the main stem loosely tied to a bamboo cane to encourage the leader to grow upright. Any side growths that appear to compete with the leader should be cut back so that all growth is centered on the main upright stem.

Box and other small-leaved evergreens are shaped by cutting back side growths as necessary to achieve the desired width of hedge. Do not trim the tops until the desired height is reached. This should be done in mid to late summer.

After about two years, the hedge can be said to be established and a routine of regular clipping can be established to maintain the hedge shape. The top of the hedge can be trimmed as fancifully as you like — castellations, topiary shapes, and so on — or simply shaped into a point or clipped flat. The contours, or batter, of the sides can be straight up and down, or tapered from narrow top to wide bottom, but the width must not be greater at the top than at the bottom; sunlight must reach all parts of the hedge evenly, which is why the batter is so important.

Old overgrown hedges of yew, beech, hawthorn, holly, and hornbeam can usually be restored to a more suitable size by hard-pruning. The removal of over-long side growth lets light into the center of the plant, which causes new healthy shoots to break from the old trunks. In the case of yew, begin by cutting back one side in the first year, then cut back the other side one or two years later, depending on how much growth the previously pruned side has made. After each pruning, feed and mulch the hedge.

Lavender hedges that have grown old and leggy may respond to hard-pruning carried out in the spring, but this is not always successful. Box is not renewable by hard-pruning, so it is better to start again with young plants.

Stilt hedges are created by keeping the trunks free of leafy branches from ground level to a desired height, usually 4-5 ft. (1.2-1.5 m) and then the leader is cut to encourage the crown to develop a network of lateral branches which are then trained horizontally by tying them into a frame of wires or canes fixed to stakes. When the lateral growth is established the training framework can be removed and the crowns pruned hard each spring to encourage fresh leafy growth.

Stooling is a pruning technique in which all the top growth of shrub is cut back to a stump or to ground level to encourage the buds forming at the base of the plant to grow and replace the old wood which has been removed. The reason for stooling a plant is to make the most of its ornamental bark or foliage, since these qualities are superior on new growth. Trees and shrubs that can be stooled to enhance their seasonal effect include colored-stem dogwoods, *Cornus sibirica*, *C. alba*, and their cultivars; *Leycesteria formosana*; ornamental-stemmed species of *Rubus*; golden-leaved elder (*Sambucus racemosa* "Plumosa Aurea"); purple-leaved elder (*S. r.* "Purpurea"); African hemp (*Sparmannia africana*); yellow-leaved Indian bean (*Catalpa bignonioides* "Aurea"); and variegated giant reed (*Arundo donax* var. *versicolor*).

Pollarding is like stooling on stilts, as it is the crown of the tree which is reduced to a frame of several stumps from which all the old stems are cut each spring. This encourages large leaves allowing the trees to provide good shade cover for paving and roadways in urban areas.

Seeing green

When deciding upon a planting scheme there are various elements to consider but form will be the primary concern. Form refers to the outline of the whole plant — what it looks like in silhouette (Fig. 1) — and is allied to the idea of habit which refers to whether the plant is fastigiate, spreading, multi-stem, or weeping (Fig. 3). Stem structure and to a lesser degree the shape of the leaves (*page 29*) help to determine the form. The style and manner in which plant forms are deployed throughout a scheme will determine the effect of the planting and define the atmosphere of the garden.

As a rule, upright vertical shapes are more emphatic than horizontal rounded shapes largely because the latter is the form most familiar to us being the one commonly encountered in nature. For this reason, designers rely on columnar forms to create eye-catching interludes in a garden plan. But for every exclamation mark in the garden, you will want to have rhythmical interludes or the effect becomes "jumpy" and these are best achieved by a repetition of forms. Garden design is mostly about manipulating the senses to influence how we perceive our surroundings, and the repetition of plant forms creates a pattern of comfortable familiarity (particularly when assembled from friendly rounded shapes). However, repeated forms must be finely balanced by a variety of other forms to avoid evoking a feeling of monotony. In the photograph *(below left)*, a sequence of clipped box balls make an emphatic statement as they roll in formation across the lawn. The regimented formality of the glossy green spheres is saved from monotony by the surrounding informal masses of various plant forms and foliage: a backdrop of trailing curtains of golden hops (*Humulus lupulus* "Aureus"), feathery fronds of male fern (*Dryopteris filix-mas*), sweet cicely (*Myrrhis odorata*) and alexanders (*Smyrnium perfoliatum*).

Similarly, but in different surroundings with different plants, the startling spikiness of a desert garden *(below right)* with linear shapes and strong verticals created by the upright cactus *Trichocereus pasacana* and the towering spikes of numerous yucca species, is relieved by a uniform scattering of spherical *Echinocactus grusonii*.

Rounded forms and strong verticals can be gained from many types of plants either naturally, as with the highly specialized leaf forms of cacti, or artificially, from clipped shrubs. Repetition of form creates a feeling of unity.

Fig.1 Tree Form

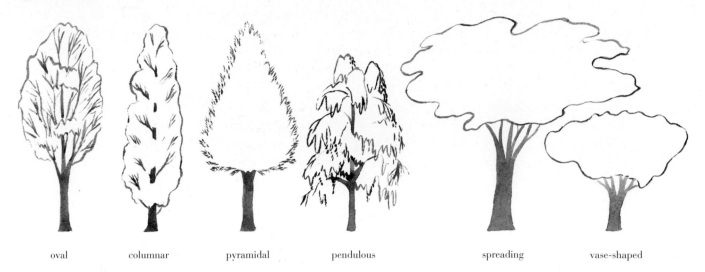

oval   columnar   pyramidal   pendulous   spreading   vase-shaped

Fig.2 Shrub Form

fastigiate   weeping   spreading   multi-stem

Fig.3 Habit

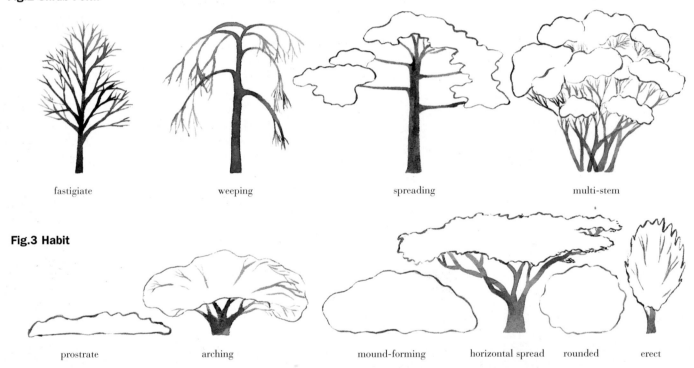

prostrate   arching   mound-forming   horizontal spread   rounded   erect

Interestingly, because this particular cactus does not have leaves, its form depends entirely on the shape of its stem and is therefore totally natural, whereas the form of the box although naturally fairly rounded is enhanced by regular clipping. These particular topiary shapes are cut from the common box species, *Buxus sempervirens*, so that the shapes are rather unexpectedly large. We most often see clipped box balls created from the dwarf cultivar, "Suffruticosa."

Specimen trees

A specimen tree does not have to mean single tree, and when trees are to be planted as markers in the landscape — something that will attract attention to a vista or area of planting — few things can be more eye-catching than a multi-stemmed tree, or a group of three or five trees all of the same variety. Generally, trees treated in this way tend to be rather ordinary subjects, like birch trees, and it is

The strident coloring of *Acer* var. *heptalobum* "Osakazuki" has the same visual impact as the breathtaking woody structure of a huge specimen of the pine, *Pseudotsuga menzieii.*

Trees with fine foliage, like *Acer palmatum* (*left*) and *Nyssa sylvatica* (*opposite*) make outstanding specimens which should be highlighted by siting them to catch the light, or else positioned so that they appear silhouetted against a darker background. Other trees, however, can be exploited by emphasizing the interesting curves and angles of their trunks and branches, as with the gnarled trunk and spreading crown of the *Acer palmatum* var. *dissectum*, (*top*) or the unique configuration of habit and foliage in a specimen evergreen like *Pinus strobus* "Pendula" (*above*).

by planting in this way that they become something special.

Single specimen trees are, however, a class apart; choice varieties or cultivars that are selected because of the unique contribution they make to the garden scheme. Most of the trees in my garden are common fruit trees. The apple orchard of heritage varieties interrupts one long axis, and the great white cherry grove makes an impact in spring and again in autumn, and in a way these features constitute specimen planting. *Liquidambar styraciflua* "Worplesdon," one of only two specimen trees in the garden, is planted at a curve in the path and marks the transi-

tion between the ornamental and wilder parts of the garden. From late summer when the leaves begin to color until the first hard frost, the tree is like a flaming beacon. At ten years old it is still growing taller, but will soon begin to compensate by increasing its girth, becoming an even more powerful magnet, pulling me spiritually and physically into the garden.

Scale remains an important consideration when selecting a specimen tree, because it would be a grave mistake to select a large tree for a small courtyard garden. Likewise, to set a small-growing specimen tree adrift in a vast country garden lawn would be unwise.

Shape is the other consideration. The shape of a tree planting refers to the overall outline of a group of plants composed from their individual forms. Tree forms are determined by the angle at which the branches are held away from the trunk: fastigiate or columnar forms occur because the angle between branch and trunk (the crotch) is narrow, and the lateral stems rising from the branches are also held at narrow angles causing the branches to be held upright or erect. The word "fastigiate" signifies this form. Many tree species will have fastigiate varieties or cultivars: *Taxus baccata* "Fastigiata" and *Betula pendula* "Fastigiata"

are commonly seen, while the evergreen Italian cypress (*Cupressus sempervirens*) is the most elegant of fastigiate trees.

Some trees will have branches held at angles near to 90°, which will give a graceful, broad, spreading form, like that of the magnificent cedar of Lebanon (*Cedrus libani*) while some will have much wider-angled crotches, giving the tree a pendulous effect; *Corylus avellana* "Pendula" is the pendulous form of hazelnut. Rounded trees with regular outlines will have a much-branched crown and no central leader (main trunk).

Pyramidal trees (*pyramidalis* in botanical parlance) have a strong leader and are much wider branching at the base than near the growing tip at the end of the leader; liquidambar has this form. Vase-shaped trees have upward-sweeping branches, so the tree has an outline like an inverted triangle; *Prunus sargentii* is an example of this form. One of the best ways to acquire an understanding of form and habit is to study the naked silhouette of deciduous trees in the depth of winter, when the landscape is reduced to sharp contrasts of dark and light. The outline and structure of the trees will be immediately apparent. It will also be easier to observe the form of various evergreens when they stand out more clearly against their deciduous companions.

If you look at the natural landscape you will probably notice how the plant forms within it reflect the forms of the terrain; pyramidal conifers seem to repeat a horizon of mountain peaks; gentle rolling landscapes find their complement in the rounded forms of deciduous trees whose broad spreading crowns seem to follow the horizon line of open ground.

Shrubs

The next layer below the tree canopy is occupied by shrubs. While a tree is a woody perennial, deciduous or evergreen, that will grow to at least 20 ft. (6 m) or more on a single stem, a shrub is defined as a woody perennial, deciduous or evergreen, that will reach a height of up to 20 ft. (6 m) and has many stems.

Like trees, shrubs have form, but because of their shorter stature (and some are very low-growing indeed) they may be prostrate or creeping, trailing or mat-forming. Others will have branches that spread out horizontally, like *Viburnum plicatum* "Mariesii," while others are erect, like *Viburnum bodnantense* "Dawn." Fig. 2 (*page 22*) shows common shrub forms.

You begin to exercise your skill as a garden designer when you assemble trees and shrubs to form the permanent framework of the garden picture. Most typically they are combined in groups that depend upon contrasting forms for their interest. For exam-

Shrubs make a major contribution to the understory planting either by unifying trees and lower level plantings of perennials and annuals or as single incidents in the landscape, like this thicket of *Rhus typhina* "Lacinata."

ple, if you have a fastigiate or erect form, a low-spreading form could be put at its base with a small rounded form to one side as a counterbalance. This grouping could then be used to establish the theme throughout the planting, and while the plants themselves might vary, their forms would not.

This theme could be used as an alternative to the formal clipped hedging described earlier, with ribbon plantings of erect and spreading shrubs forming a division of space within the garden, or forming its enclosing boundaries.

Perennials and ephemerals

Below and sometimes on a level with the shrub layer is the perennial layer, where herbaceous perennials, annuals, and biennials serve as fill-ins to the composition. Often these are linking plants, bringing together separate areas of planting. One of the most effective garden planting methods I know begins by

planting several trees in carefully prepared planting holes, at the proper distance to allow for shapely growth. The ground around the trees is heavily mulched to keep the soil surface weed-free. Once the trees are established, the shrubs are planted into carefully prepared planting holes and the soil is mulched and kept weed-free. When the shrubs are growing well — which they usually are by the following season — any turf remaining between the plants is removed, the ground is dug and manured, and perennial groundcovers are planted. Hostas and hellebores thrive in this program, as would any other plant that benefits from the cool moist soil and semi-shaded conditions of a woodland garden.

Groundcovering plants create the final layer and include many trailing plants and climbers that can look as effective carpeting the ground as they do draped on walls and fences. Groundcovers are also functional, helping to conserve soil moisture and suppress weeds.

The light tones and soft textures make a cohesive group of *Eucalyptus glaucescens*, *Acer palmatum* "Senkaki," *Sorbaria aitchisoni*, *Rosa nitida*, and *Spiraea* "Arguta," and one which stands out well against the evergreen planting behind.

The broad, coarsely textured leaves of hostas and hydrangeas combine with bold contrasts of dark and light between *Ophiopogon planiscapus* "Nigricans" and pale-leaved perennials (*left*) to make a more visually demanding scene than the restful atmosphere created by the finely textured plants in the garden above, where the tints of green are virtually all the same tone. Contrasts give emphasis to planting schemes and features, like the boundary wall of the garden (*opposite*) which is clothed in *Euonymus* "Silver Queen" and shod with *Dryopteris filix-mas* "Cristata Martindale."

Suiting the situation

Trees and shrubs are the largest group of ornamental plants, and when you sit down with a glossy gardening book it is all too easy to get sidetracked by a pretty leaf, interesting bark texture, or the siren promise of glittering autumn fruit. The best way to determine your requirements is to assess what you need from the garden, and how that can best be achieved in the context of the conditions within which you are working. You should never try to turn a dry sunny garden into a moist woodland, but trees and shrubs can create areas of cooling shade, and sculptural forms of specimen trees can be selected to add drama when viewed against the glittering sky. Grass turf is a foliage groundcover, but one which requires plenty of moisture to do well; if water shortages are a problem in your area, try gravel instead, and use hummock-forming grasses as ornamentals, combined with silver-leaved shrubs.

By adhering to a loose agenda of suiting plants to their envi-ronment you will find that the plants complement one another. By loose agenda, I mean one which permits, for example, the use of dry-shade lovers from those parts of the world which share similar minimum winter temperatures, rainfall patterns, and elevations; a strict agenda could mean that you are limiting yourself to only those plants which occur naturally in your cli-mate zone. There are too many wonderful plants to grow to be so narrow-minded.

Leaf form, texture, and color

The reason plants with similar horticultural requirements will appear cohesive is because their appearance will have adapted to accommodate conditions. For instance, plants from hot dry regions will have narrow or small and finely divided leaves to help the plant conserve water; in such areas there will be plenty of sun, so the leaves do not need a high chlorophyll content, and are often colored gray to help reflect light and reduce surface

Fig.4 Leaf Shapes

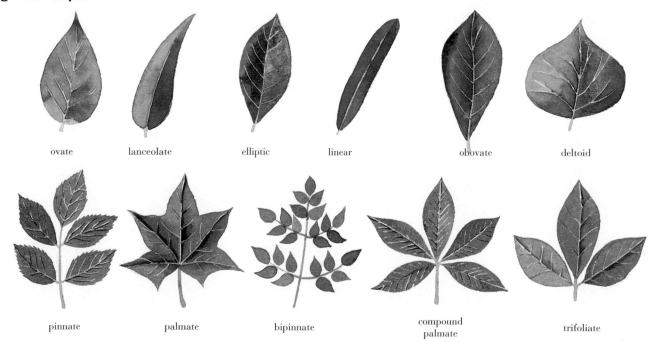

ovate   lanceolate   elliptic   linear   obovate   deltoid

pinnate   palmate   bipinnate   compound palmate   trifoliate

temperatures. Plants from hot dry countries also often have fuzzy or hairy surfaces, another feature to help cut water loss.

In the rainforest, light levels are low, so leaves must be large, and arranged along the stems as horizontally as possible in order to capture as much sunlight as they can; their shiny, waxy surface acts like the proverbial duck's back, helping to shed the vast quantities of water that can fall in minutes in a tropical downpour. The leaves of woodland shrubs and perennials from temperate zones are frequently broad and flat, facing the light source to gather the maximum amount of sun, and the plants benefit from the moisture levels provided by the sheltering leafy tree canopy overhead.

Cactus leaves are among the most specialized, with a solid structure designed to gather and hold as much water as possible during the occasional desert rains, and leaves often arranged in a pattern of concentric rings which channels the rainwater directly to the base of the plant and the root; the prickles and thorns are there to discourage predators. There are hundreds of different leaf configurations, but some of the most commonly seen forms are shown in Fig. 4 (*page 29*).

Nature has also created some leaves with variegation, although this is generally a mutation caused by a virus, or else a genetic abnormality. The more variegated a leaf is the less chlorophyll it contains and the less able it will be to absorb sunlight, which is why variegated leaves often scorch in the sun. Other leaves will have red or brown coloring, which may possibly serve as a deterrent, protecting the plant from foraging insects and herbivores. Other defense mechanisms include thorns and prickly or hairy leaves that either make the plant unpleasant to chew or else act as micro-hypodermics to inject irritants and poisons when the plant is attacked. Other plants may have toxic roots or leaves. One of the main reasons it took the tomato and the potato such a long time to catch on in Europe was that people, not knowing how to handle the unfamiliar plant, ate the

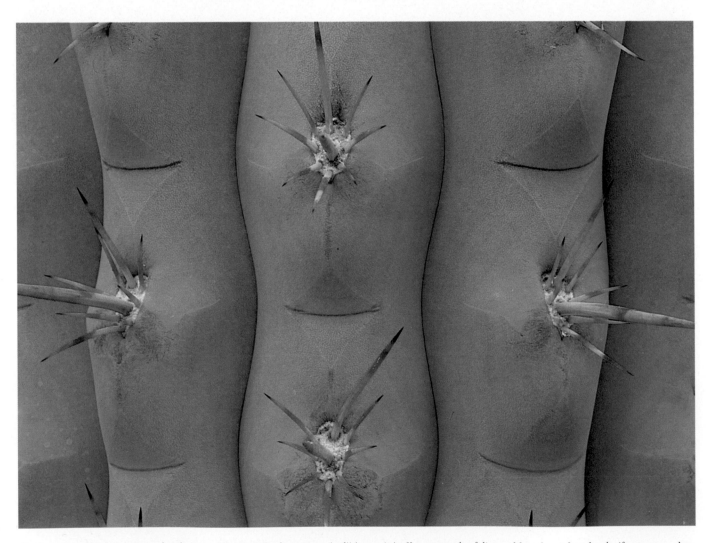

Cacti, such as this *Azureocereus hartligianus* (*above*) or *Pachycereus pringlii* (*opposite*) offer spectacular foliage; although not frost hardy, if pot-grown they can be put out in the summer garden to add an invigorating contrast to the soft foliage of familiar perennials.

Seasonal color provided by foliage is one of the gardener's greatest joys, and while some plants are known to color well, the intensity and duration of the display is dependent on less predictable weather conditions which influence the plant's performance.

foliage as well as the fruit — with bitter consequences!

Leaves are colored according to the levels of certain pigments they contain which are an important aid to photosynthesis. The main one, and most efficient for the photosynthetic process, is chlorophyll, and the greener the leaf the higher the chlorophyll content. Red and dark mahogany brown leaves contain a higher proportion of a vinous red pigment, anthocyanin. Carotene is an orange pigment and xanthrophyll pigments range from yellow to neutral. The levels of these pigments in a leaf determine whether it is acid green, butter yellow, blue-green, or chocolate brown.

Autumn color is the result of a plant's response to seasonal changes. This can happen very suddenly or quite gradually depending on the plant and what the weather is like as the plant begins to shut down for winter, at which time it concentrates its energy on food storage rather than production. The specimen *Liquidambar styraciflua* "Worplesdon" in my garden colors slowly, turning at first a dirty green, but then the red pigments come to the fore as the chlorophyll-rich part of the leaf fades. By mid-autumn the whole tree is rich burgundy red, with hints of flame orange. This happens regardless of the weather. The other specimen tree, *Betula maximowicziana*, is entirely dependent on the weather for any autumn glory. In fact, I had begun to wonder why I had planted it at all, until one autumn when the days remained dry and sunny and the nights became very cold. The leaves continued food production in the daytime, but the transfer to storage was slowed by the cold night temperatures. The tree turned the most stunning and intense egg yolk yellow, and each large, heart-shaped leaf fluttered brilliantly against the blue sky. I had simply forgotten how perfect an autumn tree it

The larger the leaf the coarser the texture will appear. *Left*, the clearly defined medium-sized leaves of *Epimedium × perralchicum* present a more refined appearance than the robust oversize foliage of *Rodgersia podophylla* and *Lysichiton americanus*, *right*.

was, given the optimum autumn conditions for good color comprising dry, sunny days and cold nights. And when the leaves dropped, they did so all at the same time, leaving a pool of sunshine on the ground.

Perennial plants also have autumn color attributes, but to a lesser extent than trees. Sometimes hostas can hold their foliage intact through a dry autumn and turn butter yellow. Ornamental grasses turn biscuity beige or tawny gold as the pigments fade. Some foliage perennials that have a reddish cast, for example bergenias and heuchera, will become redder as the weather gets colder. Gold variegations on evergreens like holly, elaeagnus and box seem to become richer in the winter, but that may be more to do with the fact that there is little competition from other plants, many of which will have retreated below ground, in the bright-color stakes.

Foliage and planting design

In addition to the form and habit of a plant, the other physical characteristics which will influence how the plants are used in garden design are texture and color.

Textures can be described as fine, medium or coarse, matte, glossy, heavy or light and combinations of these qualities will further define the plant's texture. For instance, a common cherry laurel with its broad shiny leaves held stiffly away from the stems could be described as coarse and glossy; rosemary would be seen as fine and matte. If a leaf is covered in fine hairs, it will absorb light and so have a softer look. Thus, these descriptive attributes are determined by the physical characteristics of the leaves, stems, and bark, how they relate to one another, and how light is absorbed or reflected by their surfaces.

Top. Santolina neapolitana "Edward Bowles" has finely cut, dense silvery foliage which gives it a delicate soft focus quality in contrast to the coarser appearance of the *Sedum spectabile* in the background. *Above.* Fairly smooth broad flat leaves, like those of *Peltiphyllum*, will reflect light while deeply textured leaves like those of the chinese cabbage "Nagaoke," *right*, absorb it.

As a general rule, the larger the leaf and heavier the branch the coarser the appearance of the plant. But loose, open foliage will also make the plant look coarse. Small-leaved plants, like box, that have dense foliage will appear softer.

The form of the individual leaves will also influence the appearance of the plant, with compound leaves appearing softer than large simple leaves. Just think of a maidenhair fern frond; what could be softer and finer than its complex leaves made of tiny individual leaflets on dark wiry stems? Conversely, a hart's tongue fern with its single, broad, flat leaf appears coarse by comparison.

In garden design, the textural qualities of foliage plants and their relationship in plant groupings should be carefully considered. Soft matte textures, like that of yew, beech, or hornbeam,

Top. Edible plants, like the mustard greens "Red Giant" and pak choi cabbage often have arresting foliage and can be used as filler plants in the garden. *Above.* Contrasts give emphasis; here rounded hosta leaves are set against the strap-like foliage of crocosmia and wands of willow gentian. *Right.* Similarly, the upright habit of the fern fronds is enhanced by the spread leaves of the rodgersia.

make the best backdrops for showing off other flower or foliage plants, because their dense shadowy quality makes a perfect low-key partner; glossy, coarse holly would be too assertive and distract attention from the foreground plantings. However, to emphasize a boundary, or to create an attention-getting device, holly would be hard to better.

Contrasts of texture, size, and shape are what make plant

groupings lively and interesting to look at; they hold our attention by the quality of the pattern they create. But a grouping must be executed thoughtfully; a jumble of many different plants will look just that. Simplicity is the key to successful planting.

Contrasts should never be played out simply as jarring juxtapositions; putting a spiky fastigiate tree with a low soft rounded shrub is too abrupt a transition. Add a loose open shape, however, and the composition is much more pleasing because it is easier on the eye.

Northern-hemisphere gardeners are used to soft even shapes and flowing lines, which is why, when viewing a tropical garden planted with spiky palms, bristling with cacti, padded out with succulents and glowing with glossy broad-leaved foliage plants in every shape and size, we find the whole scene quite spellbinding. It may, in part, be a gardener's version of "the grass is always greener," but the theatrical effects of plants like this can be used to give drama to our tame temperate gardens. Not all gardeners have the wherewithal to grow true exotics — heated greenhouses do not come cheap. Some plants we use, however, like the giant *Gunnera manicata*, have exotic-looking leaves, as do the ferny fronds of the tree of heaven (*Ailanthus altissima*). Bamboo is exotic by nature, but hardy enough in most gardens to be used to good effect. When plants like this are employed, it should be done to make a point — to attract attention to a part of the garden — rather than deploying them wherever the

opportunity presents itself. In the same way, focal points benefit from having a strongly patterned foliage plant at the epicenter. A clutch of sumac (*Rhus typhina*) planted against a light background, or on a high point where the bent and crooked branches and palm-like leaves will be silhouetted against the sky, makes good use of this plant's highly individual characteristics. One of the most beautiful trees is the variegated dogwood (*Cornus controversa* "Variegata"), which has small leaves that are variegated creamy white with branches held in ascending tiers like a silvery pagoda. I have seen this tree planted at the foot of a gently rising slope in a woodland garden. Planted to be center-stage as one descends the main axial path into the garden, its spreading branches reach out, drawing you ever further into the leafy shadows along the grassy ride leading through the garden. It is the most effective and dramatic visual statement, and sets the tone for the entire garden. From that moment you know that every plant will have been placed with a great deal of careful thought.

Above. Some plants are outstanding simply because of their unfamiliar, hence exotic, appearance and coloring, like this English garden tropical border planted with canna lilies, ricinus, jacaranda, and a host of other half-hardy plants. *Opposite.* A few plants have stand-alone elegance and, like the variegated dogwood *Cornus controversa* "Variegata" illustrated here, should be given focal point status.

Color is an emotive issue in more ways than just encouraging highly charged discussions between gardeners — "I can't stand purple," "One more white garden and I'll scream." Color influences our lives in so many ways. Gray skies encourage gloom; sunshine cheers. Pink calms, yet red is a signal to anger. And green cools and soothes the soul.

Monochromatic color schemes are a popular device, as in the famous white garden at Sissinghurst or Hidcote's red borders. Green gardens are less common although in Japan, gardens which depend on a naturalistic use of foliage are central to the architectural content of temple enclosures. Even domestic gardens, in a land-poor country, are miniature representations of the natural woodland of mountain and valley. Moss gardens are an extreme example of a monochromatic foliage garden. The groundcover is a sheath of mosses and lichens, shaded by carefully pruned pines and clumps of bamboo; ornament is minimal and the interest is held entirely by the spirituality of the scene.

The Italian Renaissance garden is, perhaps, a more familiar monochromatic garden, where clipped hedges and carefully pruned trees serve to focus all of our attention on the architecture of the villa, the statuary, and the hard-landscaping features of the garden itself. As in a moss garden, few species are used. Usually there is box, clipped into tight low hedges or topiary; evergreen oak (*Quercus ilex*) is used along with bay (*Laurus nobilis*) and cypress (*Cupressus sempervirens*) to make background and major boundary hedges. Cypress and umbrella pines make pronounced vertical accents. The groundcovering plants are typically ivy and rough grass, but the turf is generally a tapestry of "weeds" — plantains, prunella, thyme, ajuga, creeping mints, and all sorts of little-leaved plants that we would be quite happy to cultivate in borders, but break our backs removing from the lawn. Highly formalized, architectural gardens in the Italianate style have an intellectual repose in the unfolding order and geometry of the landscape.

Monochromatic color schemes are popular in gardens. *Left*. White variegated hostas underpin white violas and tulips "White Dream" and "Maureen." *Right*.
Onopordum acanthium is thrown into sharp relief by the filmy flowers of *Crambe cordifolia* and the rose "Jacqueline Du Pré."

Harmonies and contrasts can be developed out of a monochromatic scheme, because although a garden is green, there are many different shades of green, ranging from the silvery gray-green *Artemisia canescens* to the midnight green of *Ophiopogon planiscapsus* "Nigrescens." The color wheel shown here is an indication of the range of colors available when planning a foliage garden.

A color harmony occurs when adjacent colors in the color wheel are used together. Thus, on the true color wheel, where red, blue, and yellow are the primary colors, the harmonies would be created by red, purple, and blue; blue, green, and yellow; red, orange, and yellow; red, purple, and orange and so on. Two colors would probably dominate while the third color would

Shades of green can be organized in a manner similar to the true color wheel as there are blue-greens, yellow-greens, and red-greens and corresponding hues in between. Just as the true color wheel is the basis for flower planting schemes, so the "green wheel" can be used to organize foliage, bark, and berry for genuine year-round color in the garden. *Clockwise from top left corner*, the plants are: *Carya ovata* (butter yellow); *Helichrysum petiolare* "Limelight" (silvery pale yellow); *Artemesia ludoviciana* "Silver Queen" (silver gray); *Elymus magellanicus* (pale gray); *Hosta sieboldiana* var *elegans* (slate gray); *Eryngium bourgatii* "Oxford Blue" (blue violet); *Ajuga reptans* "Atropurpurea" (purple); *Ophiopogon planiscapus* "Nigrescens" (black green); *Rodgersia podophylla* (brown); *Magnolia grandiflora* (dark green/khaki); *Gunnera manicata* (mid-green); *Lysimachia nummularia* "Aurea" (acid yellow).

be used to lift the scheme. This can be translated to the green color wheel so that, for example, silver gray (*Stachys byzantina* "Cotton Boll"), pale dove gray (*Lychnis coronaria* "Alba"), and silvery yellow (*Verbascum pulverulentum*) could be blended, or ruddy purple (*Vitis vinifera* "Purpurea") with dark vinous green (*Salvia officinalis* "Purpurea") and a touch of rusty brown (*Carex comans* Bronze Form). Working with tints of green is perhaps slightly more tricky as the color bias is less obvious, but experience is a great teacher, and you will soon know how to see green in all its variety.

Color contrasts rely on matching complementary hues — colors that are opposite each other on the wheel. On a true wheel it would put purple and yellow, blue and orange, and red and green together. On the green wheel, it would blend slate and pale gray with butter yellow or silver gray and yellow with dark purple.

Add in variegated plants or colored stems and berries and the whole exercise takes on another dimension, yet these plants will have a predominant hue, be it yellow, white, red, blue, or purple, and so can be associated with the appropriate segment of the green wheel.

The other way to use color is to follow nature's lead. If you observe the changing seasons you will notice that each part of the year carries its own color scheme. Early spring is full of acid yellows, dark purples, and vivid greens as the fresh young foliage unfurls. In the earliest part of the year a planting of dwarf conifer *Pinus mugo* "Ophir," *Cornus stolonifera* "Flaviramea," *Ajuga reptans* "Catlin's Giant," and yellow- and green-variegated *Acorus gramineus* "Ogon" would bring all these colors together. As summer moves in, the colors deepen, losing freshness until the end of the season brings in the fiery crimsons and honey and amber tones of ripening fields of grain. An unsprayed field of summer wheat sprinkled with crimson poppies is one of nature's most beautiful garments; the fine-leaved grass *Stipa tenuissima* fades to silky beige and planted with the yellow-daisy-flowered *Anthemis tinctoria* "E. C. Buxton"

 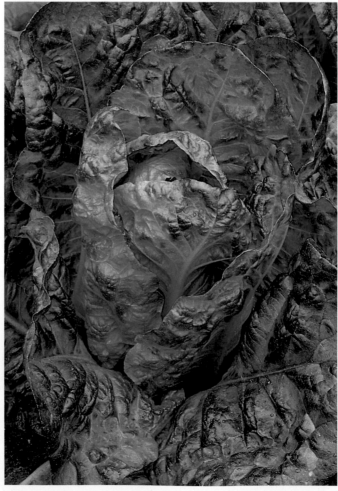

Left. Many yellow-leaved plants scorch in sunlight; the grass *Milium effusum* "Aureum," seen here with *Hosta fortunei* var *albopicta* and the orange-flowered hybrid of *Trollius chinensis* will brighten a semi-shaded corner. *Right.* Sunlight deepens the red coloring of the ornamental lettuce "Petite Rouge."

Contrasting color schemes are notoriously tricky, evoking strong prejudices in the eye of the beholder. Particularly sensitive is the use of magenta red and saturated orange, as here in the cabbage "Christmas Mix" planted with pumpkin colored *Calendula* "Orange King."

would recall this summer picture. Winter is monotone-time, when charcoal-dark branches are silhouetted against gray skies and evergreen shrubs and trees dominate the garden. A simple statement, like a well-branched specimen of *Betula nigra* "Heritage," with its characteristic white bark lightly flushed with buff-apricot tints, silhouetted against the dark mass of a tight-clipped yew hedge, best captures winter's essence.

Just as the form and textures of a foliage plant can be used to manipulate our experience of the landscape, so can the way we use color influence how we perceive a garden. There are certain characteristics of color that can be used to set a mood, visually alter the perspective, or capture the attention. In the context of planting a foliage garden, it is well to remember that turgid, muddy colors can be fairly oppressive and so should be used sparingly, possibly as accents to brighter schemes. By using a predominance of gray or silver plants you can attempt to re-create a corner of the Mediterranean, but remember that

in sunny regions the soft foliage colors are set off by vivid flowers. In western gardens, a solidly emerald green garden modeled on a Japanese woodland will benefit from having touches of white, cream and ivory introduced in leaf variegations and flower color.

Design alternatives

There are many ways to approach the design of a garden that relies heavily on foliage rather than flowers. If all the chat about color, scale, and form is too dry for your tastes, it might be more fun to choose an esoteric theme and collect the plants around that idea. One of England's greatest plantsmen, E. A. Bowles, had at his garden at Myddleton House a corner devoted to botanical oddities which he dubbed "the lunatic asylum." A friend of mine is developing a "torture corner" devoted to plants with naturally twisted, gnarled, or faciated (flattened) stems,

Santolina "Lemon Queen," rosemary, box, and artemisia are used to form the interlaced threads of a herbal knot, a device that is one of the oldest uses of foliage plants in garden design; the woven effect is achieved by clipping the hedge to differing heights.

grotesque thorns or hideous smells — not a part of the garden in which to linger. Brown-leaved plants would offer plenty of scope, from the splendid *Macleaya cordata* which can reach towering heights up to 8 ft. (2.4 m), to the ground-covering *Geranium sessiliflorum novae-zelandiae* "Nigricans." Macleaya is one of the best herbaceous perennials for foliage display. The leaves are glaucous gray touched with copper and the flower plumes are soft buff pink. It is quite invasive: once you have it you always will, and it runs around on its widely travelling roots. However, it is easy to pull up where it is not wanted and should be in every foliage garden worthy of the name.

Geranium sessiliflorum novae-zelandiae "Nigricans" is another easy mover, and one of the best for brown foliage. The flowers are like little white stars and the whole thing is perfectly sweet. There are many hardy geraniums that have good foliage and are worth collecting. I would start with *Geranium robertianum*, the common herb robert of hedgerows and old herbals. The leaves are deeply cut and so have a light lacy appearance, and as the season advances towards autumn, the emerald green coloring turns deep ruby-red. They have a pungent resinous scent and all summer the plants are covered in little pink star-like flowers. There is a white-flowered cultivar "Album," which is even more desirable. The plant throws its stems about, weaving in and out

of neighboring plants. It is a freely self-seeding annual. *G. macrorrhizum* "Ingwersen's Variety" has a similar resinous scent, but the leaves are rounded and have a slightly felted surface, and color well in autumn. Used in mass plantings as groundcover beneath a stilt-hedge it makes an impressive sight. *G. renardii* is not particularly scented, but the leaves are soft gray-green and the plant shapes up into a pleasing mound that is covered in small white flowers in summer.

And if that's not enough, there are all the scented pelargoniums, tender relatives of the hardy clan, but with leaves that you select first for their scent and second for their interesting appearance. One of the most highly perfumed, and a favorite with Victorian conservatory gardeners, is "Mabel Grey." The leaves have the strongest citrus scent and the stiff, serrated leaves look like doll-size fans. "Chocolate Peppermint" is deeply lobed, has a felted surface and the center of each leaf is marked with a deep maroon chocolatey blotch. "Acushla" has thumbnail-sized pearly green foliage strongly smelling of apples and incense: "Odoratissimum" has a sandalwood and orange perfume and *Pelargonium crispum* "Variegatum" has tiny ruffled leaves splashed with cream and scented of peppermint. There are more, so you could become obsessive, which I have. Because they are not hardy, my scented geraniums are housed in pots which stand

The lemon balm, *Melissa officinalis* "Aurea," is variegated with splashes of bright yellow, particularly useful for lifting a dark corner.

out on the terrace during the summer. There, amidst the orange, lemon, and olive trees which are also pot-grown, they bask in whatever sun comes our way, trying — and usually succeeding — to remind me of favorite Tuscan gardens. For winter, they are moved to the greenhouse and there kept frost-free, and when spring rolls around, the plants are repotted or given fresh soil mix and cut back to encourage a lush new growth of scented leaves. Their curious textures, odd shapes and attractive markings invite you to touch the leaves, and so release the scent.

Herb gardens

Scented foliage plants are varied and beautiful, and herb gardens are in essence scented foliage gardens. Try to look beyond their use as a flavoring or a remedy and learn to regard the plants as ornamental shrubs, herbaceous perennials, or annuals. Study their form, habit, and the textures and colors of individual leaves and you will soon see the potential for taking herbs into the ornamental garden.

Few herb gardens are without lavender, and with good reason. Every part of the plant has the characteristic resinous sweet perfume. Lavender flowers come in white and shades of purple and pink to rose; cultivars from New Zealand like the pink-flowered *Lavandula* "Marshwood" and dark red-purple *L.* "Helmsdale"

are pungently scented introductions. The foliage is typically linear and felt-soft in varying shades of gray; *L.* "Sawyers" has wider and more silvery gray leaves than some of the new cultivars; the species *L. lanata* has particularly soft woolly leaves and *L. canariensis* and *L. dentata* are distinctly serrate.

Fine-textured and tall-growing fennel (*Foeniculum vulgare*) is especially beautiful as a fill-in plant among roses and delphiniums; the bronze-leaved fennel (*F. v. purpureum*) is so often seen in this context that it is easy to forget about the clear coloring of common green fennel. It is perennial but will also seed around freely. Dill (*Anethum graveolens*) is another feathery textured herb, but it grows to only about 18 in. (45 cm) so should be saved for use among shorter growing annuals; I like it with the golden-stiped grass *Molinia caerulea caerulea* "Variegata" and lady's mantle (*Alchemilla mollis*). Lemon balm (*Melissa officinalis*) is a rapid groundcover, scented highly of citrus; the cultivar "All Gold" has pure yellow leaves and should be shaded from the midday sun since it will scorch.

The fern-like foliage of sweet cicely (*Myrrhis odorata*) gives the herb a fine texture. It is clear green, tall-growing and makes a good filler plant with herbaceous flowers.

Several perennial herbs are excellent architectural plants — ones that have strong and determined outlines that can be used

as focal points in the garden. Foremost is doubtless the cardoon *Cynara cardunculus*. It looks very like a globe artichoke, but the cardoon's huge leaves are more deeply lobed and each lobe more finely laciniated, and more silvery gray. It begins to push through the ground in early spring, and that is when it can be lifted, divided (it is easily propagated by offsets), and replanted, which should be done regularly since young plants provide better foliage. It will soon make a vast clump of arching gray leaves up to 4 ft. (1.2 m) across, eventually throwing up an erect, thistle-headed flower. This should be removed as the foliage will begin to deteriorate if the cardoon is allowed to flower; cut the stem as near to the base of the plant as possible.

The compound leaves of the tall-growing lovage (*Levisticum officinale*) are dark green, glossy, and quite coarse in appearance. Angelica (*Angelica archangelica*) has similar textures and gloss but the leaves are paler green and slightly larger than lovage. The stems and leaves of *A. gigas* are tinged with port-purple.

Laurus nobilis, the ever popular bay tree, is often used to make ornamental standards and geometric topiary since the stiff green leaves hold the shape well. The green is rather a dull mid-tone, so if you want the formal shaping but in a bolder color, try the cultivar *L. n.* "Aurea," which has good golden-green leaves. They do scorch in full sun so the plant needs to be in a spot that is semi-shaded when the sun is at its height; the white variegation of "Morroway Silver" makes the foliage look as though it has been sprayed with bleach.

Variegation

Variegation holds particular fascination for some plant collectors as well as for designers — a splash of bright yellow in a dark corner is a welcome sight. But to my eye — and all these considerations are highly personal anyway — variegation in moderation is best. It is easy to overdo, since the very nature of variegation removes some of the structural definition of a plant and thus if every plant used in a scheme were to be variegated

Opposite. Some variegated plants carry their coloring along the edges of the leaves like *Phlox paniculata* "Norah Leigh" and spear-leafed *Sisyrinchium striatum*. Variegation permits some playful juxtapositions in a planting scheme, as with this cheerful display of the variegated *Euonymus* "Emerald Gaiety" partnered with brightly colored *Ribes sanguineum* "Brocklebankii" (*above*).

the effect could be nothing more than a fuzzy confusion of blotched and spattered leaves. Used with discretion, however, variegation can lift a planting scheme from the ordinary to the exceptional.

I like to see variegation at ground level because then the leaves become part of a tapestry covering the soil. Lamiums provide some of the finest bright colorings for moist soils in semi-shade. *Lamium galeobdolon* "Hermann's Pride" has bright silver leaves netted with green veining; *L. g.* "Silberteppich" ("Silver Carpet") is more purely silver-leaved. *L. maculatum* "White Nancy" has white flowers and silver leaves while the cultivar *L. m.* "Aureum" has bright budgerigar-yellow foliage with a silver flash down the midrib vein; it looks spectacular used with Bowles' golden grass (*Carex elata* "Aurea") and other plants whose foliage tends towards yellow/green.

Pulmonarias are good groundcovers in moisture-retentive soil in part shade; the leaf shapes range from shapely ovals to narrow tapering as seen in the fine cultivar *Pulmonaria longifolia* "Bertram Anderson." Variegation usually appears as silver blotching and spotting, but *P. rubra* "David Ward" has soft gray-green leaves edged with cream.

Vinca major "Variegata" always catches my eye, with the bold yellow and green splashes covering the glossy oval leaves. It spreads rapidly, rooting wherever it touches. *Vinca minor* "Argenteovariegata" has faint white edging and splashes at the tips of the leaves, as does *Pachysandra terminalis* "Variegata," another vigorous groundcover for semi- or full shade.

The rounded silvery leaves of *Saxifraga stolonifera* are covered in tiny hairs, and are tinged with the ruddy red coloring of the creeping stolons by which the plant will colonize moist, shady spots in the garden. In summer tall-growing flower stems up to 18 in. (45 cm) tall shoot skywards, bearing dangling white moth-like flowers; a stunning plant for gardens, hardy to zone 6, but usually seen on the kitchen windowsill. Do yourself a favor and move it to the garden if you can.

Many good foliage plants have prettily tinted berries and should be included in a planting scheme for the contribution they make to late season color: *left* is the yellow fruit of *Ilex aquifolium* "Bacciflava"; *right* the rosy berries of *Sorbus* "Kirsten Pink"; and *opposite*, the familiar crimson fruit of *Cotoneaster marquandii*.

The sagittate leaves of *Arum italicum italicum* "Marmoratum" are rich glossy green with the network of veins boldly picked out in silvery cream. From the early spring to midsummer the leaves look terrific, especially when used to make groundcovering clumps with hosta and hellebore. When the leaves have fallen away, the bold spikes of bright red berries poking through the mulch really do cheer a drab scene.

There are many variegated trees, but if you are planning on planting one, go for the best. Apart from the dogwood described earlier, the creamy variegated oak *Quercus cerris* "Argenteovariegata" is a stunner.

Berries

After foliage and bark, berries are the remaining attribute that can increase a plant's worth in the garden, brightening up the dull parts of the year with vivid tints of red, yellow and orange, sapphire blue and ebony black. But berry color is as transient as that of the flowers that precede it, and there are times when it will only last as long as it takes a flock of birds to strip the shrub of its jewels. Nature-lovers will, therefore, find selecting shrubs for berried treasure doubly rewarding, since they will be stocking the food cupboard for local fauna.

Holly and cotoneaster are probably the most widely known and widely grown berry shrubs, but pyracantha (firethorn) and

snowberry are also hugely popular. Hot-colored berries are the speciality of *Pyracantha coccinea*, and follow on from the sweet-scented clusters of tiny white flowers that shroud the plant in spring. Pyracanthas are frequently trained as wall shrubs and can be pruned to achieve ornamental latticework effects. *P. rogersiana*, *P.* "Orange Glow" and the upright-growing *P. coccinea* "Lalandei" have burnt-orange berries, and the former has a yellow-berried form, *P. rogersiana f. flava*. Pyracantha will grow anywhere and most are hardy to 5° F (-15° C). However, for orange berries the sea buckthorn *Hippophae rhamnoides* is hard to better, although to grow it you need poor soil and a sunny spot. It grows naturally in coastal dunes and sandy soils of dry river beds from England to northwest China and its sturdy rounded shape, growing up to 30 ft. (10 m), can withstand strong winds, with or without salt. The stiff, narrow foliage is silvery gray-green and the whole plant has a wiry rugged look. The little spring flowers are followed by rusty orange berries that hug the stems along their length — provided you have planted both male and female.

The snowberry (*Symphoricarpos albus*) makes a small mounding shrub up to 4 ft. (1.2 m). The arching stems carry pale pink flowers in spring which then form the clusters of pearly white berries that dangle among the tangled brown stems. It is a suckering, rather uninteresting shrub for most of the year,

quite hardy and needs moist soil. It has a cousin, *S. × chenaultii*, that has rosy pink berries and *S. × doorenbosii* "Mother of Pearl" has berries streaked and splashed with cream, pink, and rose.

The heavenly bamboo *Nandina domestica* is good value all year, with the leaves changing from pinkish-brown juvenile coloring through dark green and finally to a rich purplish sepia in autumn, studded with clusters of glistening ruby-red fruit. When grown well it makes a spectacular low hedge. Bright red berries are an occasional feature of the elderberry *Sambucus racemosa* "Tenuifolia"; it makes a low mounding shrub with a filmy appearance from the extremely narrow leaves which are tinged with purple when young.

Blue berries are attention-getters and the bluest is the sapphire berry (*Symplocos paniculata*). The deciduous leaves are heavily textured, glossy green ovals and the flowers appear like fuzzy white snowballs followed by the shining blue berries. This loose-growing shrub needs acid soil in sun or shade and will grow to 15 ft. (4.5 m), so use it for boundary planting. Some viburnums have bright grapey-blue berries; *V. davidii* is especially good, with berry clusters held above the attractive evergreen foliage. *Drimys lanceolata* is a winter-flowering evergreen that has narrow tapering leaves and glittering little black fruit; the leaves and bark are scented of cinnamon and the flowers have a similar spiciness that warms the winter breeze. *Cornus sanguinea* has brick-red autumn leaves and clusters of shiny blueberry-black fruit.

Mahonias have holly-like compound leaves, and the racemes of sweet-scented flowers, reminiscent of lily-of-the-valley, are followed by sprays of bloomy blue fruit. The holly grape (*Mahonia aquifolium*) has good autumn color, with the leaves becoming flushed with coppery purple, and the blue-black fruit makes delicious jelly that has an invigorating tanginess.

Rosehips are famously useful for jelly-making and have traditionally been used to make a health-giving syrup as they contain a large amount of vitamin C. The most lusciously hipped rose is the *R. rugosa* cultivar "Scabrosa." The foliage has the rugged texture and rich autumn gold coloring of other rugosas, and the flowers appear over an incredibly long season. A hedge of this rose is dazzling clothed in autumn colors with the cherry-pink flowers and huge crab apple-sized crimson hips all vying for attention together. It will sucker and spread easily, and can be sheared back in the late winter or early spring to ready it for the next extravaganza. *R. nutkana* "Plena" is a vigorous, upright-growing rose; in autumn the current season's growth and the abundant clusters of little round hips take on a rich color so that the plant appears dipped upside-down in red paint.

Tassels

Tassels are another aspect of plant interest that is worth mentioning. The branches of the hazelnut trees in the old boundary hedge that is part of my garden are adorned with buttery-yellow tassels in late

Flowers fade to berries and seedheads, which are the main reproductive part of a plant; like the seeds of *Hordeum jubatum*, *left*, and *Pulsatilla vulgaris*, *right*, they can also be curiously attractive.

Tassels and catkins are underappreciated, yet their languorous shape and the way they catch the weak light in autumn or spring can bring a dull planting scheme to life.

winter to early spring and have spread themselves among the shiny thickets of emerald-green holly. A few scarlet berries still dot the holly trees at this time and the picture could not be prettier.

The common hazelnut (*Corylus avellana*) is tasseled, and there is also *C. a.* "Contorta" which has crazily twisted stems and splendid clusters of soft white tassels; it is hard to look at this tree with any degree of comfort in summer since the leaves are all scrunched and wrinkled too, but winter nakedness and maturity improve it no end.

Itea ilicifolia is an evergreen that carries its flowers at the end of summer. They are sweetly scented and carried in tiny whorls around the long dangling tassels. It does best against a warm wall. *Garrya elliptica* is hardy but still needs full sun and shelter in winter to protect its winter-flowering tassels and leathery

evergreen foliage from frost damage. When well grown it looks most handsome, with the silvery felting on the undersides of the leaves setting off the pale green catkins to perfection. The cultivar *G. a.* "James Roof" produces especially fine catkins as long as 12 in. (30 cm) in good conditions.

Catkins are the main feature of the willow tribe; one of the most pleasing, *Salix lanata*, has round, heavily felted gray leaves that are held in tight bunches close to the stiff dark stems. The catkins are short stubby little caterpillars held upright like candles in silver sconces. *S. magnifica* is altogether more spectacular, making a deciduous shrub up to 20 ft. (6 m) with leathery green oval leaves and female catkins up to 12 in. (30 cm) long. The male catkins, held upright from the sinuous spreading branches, are half that length and tinged with red at the tips when young.

THE GARDENS

The ideal way to learn about garden design and planting is to look at how other people have approached the subject, and this can best be achieved by visiting gardens in your area, noting the plants that particularly interest you and talking to the gardeners. Not only will you be able to learn from their successes, you will also be able to learn from their failures!

The ten gardens on these pages make particularly good use of foliage, and demonstrate the points I have made in earlier sections about borrowing from nature to create gardens that are in harmony with their surroundings. The plans which accompany them are meant as suggested rough guides to the planting schemes; they are not intended to be rigid recipes. Instead, allow them to encourage you to investigate the many different species and cultivars within a genus.

Look and learn. Take in the broad garden picture, then narrow your focus down to the details of plant groupings, individual plants, and finally the plant structure of leaf, bark, and berry.

A garden appears to be painted in monochrome across winter's broad canvas, but the glitter of iced branches and frosted forms of evergreens and bare-stemmed deciduous shrubs emphasize the three-dimensional nature of a garden.

A winter garden

At Wollerton Old Hall in Shropshire, England, Lesley Jenkins has used foliage plants to provide interest in the garden throughout the year as well as to give the design structure. Beech hedges divide the space into distinct areas, the warm caramel brown color of the spent foliage providing a mid-tone to the dark inky greens of topiary yew and glossy emerald of clipped box edgings. These three shrubs are widely used as structural plants.

Common European beech (*Fagus sylvatica*) is a robust plant that when left to its own devices makes a graceful large tree, but it is also amenable to a yearly clipping to make a fine decorative hedge. Although deciduous, the leaves do cling to the branches and only drop when the new foliage begins to appear in the spring, so a beech hedge has a quasi-evergreen quality and for some gardens this can be an advantage — as in this garden, where the ribbons of golden brown tie the various units together. However, I find that the brown leaves begin to look a bit tired by the end of winter, and I prefer hornbeam (*Carpinus betulus*) for this type of hedging. It drops its leaves in autumn, but a mature hedge provides a dense thicket of wiry branches. The juvenile foliage is acid green and has a pleasing

Above. Plants used to create a parterre similar to the one at Wollerton Old Hall are: I Clipped box balls; II Box hedge; III *Thymus pseudolanuginosus*; IV *Ilex aquifolium* "Silver Queen"; V *Viola* "Boughton Blue"; VI *Alchemilla mollis*; VII *Saxifraga* "London Pride"; VIII Turf; IX Clipped yew cones; X Beech hedge; XI *Acaena saccaticupula* "Blue Haze";
Left. In summer the topiary shapes bring focus to the flower-filled enclosed garden. But it is the winter frost that enhances the solid evergreen forms, bringing them a sculptural quality that remains even under a thick blanket of snow.

corrugated texture adding further interest as if in compensation for its winter nakedness.

The other beech which is occasionally used for hedging is *Fagus sylvatica purpurea*, the copper or purple beech, but a little of this coloring goes a long way, and a purple hedge used throughout a garden could be overwhelming.

In the parterre the beech hedge picks up the color of the herring-bone brick paving so that the garden floor and walls are unified by color. At the center a strong vertical accent is given by the lollipop standard of a clipped variegated holly, *Ilex aquifolium* "Silver Queen," which in spite of its name is male (no berries) and has

leaves edged with creamy yellow. This holly sometimes throws out branches on which the leaves are pure glistening yellow. *I. a.* "Golden Milkboy" (male) has its variegation in reverse with the gold splash at the center of the leaf. *I. a.* "Ferox Argentea" is the creamy yellow variegated hedgehog holly with spines along the upper surface of the leaf, giving a shrub a curious "woolly" appearance when viewed from a distance. Even where holly is native and regarded as 100 per cent hardy, a severely cold winter can denude a tree. Thus, if your garden is in a region where freezing winters are prolonged, growing a holly as a containered ornamental is an option worth considering, since it can be moved to shelter before winter sets in. Any of the clones from *I. × meserveae*, for example, I. m. "Blue Angel," and I. m. "Goliath," are very hardy and will keep their glossy green leaves throughout the coldest winter.

However, if you want to grow holly and won't mind the loss of leaves, go for the deciduous holly *Ilex verticilliata*, which has ruby-red berries glittering along naked branches throughout the winter; *I. v. aurantiaca* has orange berries and is hardy enough for continental winters.

While we're thinking of hardiness, *Ilex crenata* offers cold-climate gardeners a selection of small-leaved varieties that are good substitutes for box where a low clipped hedge is needed. *I. c.*

"Mariesii" has dainty round leaves densely packed along stubby stems; *I. c.* "Convexa" has small leaves with turned-under edges, hence the name; *I. c.* "Sentinel" looks most like box; and *I. c.* "Variegata" is mottled with sunny yellow.

Buxus sempervirens is common box, the sort to grow for large hedging or topiary work; *B. s.* "Suffruticosa" is dwarf box and should be used for tight, low edgings and container-grown topiary like the clipped balls in terracotta pots decorating the parterre at Wollerton Old Hall. Clipping should be done in late summer and the hedges given an annual mulch in early spring, when they should also be fed with a general-purpose fertilizer to prevent bald patches from developing, which can occur with such rigorous regular pruning. Unless you have a particularly accurate eye, it is advisable to use a guide to ensure that levels are maintained. In one intricate Italian garden near Florence, a spider's web of strings and stakes overlays the box garden at clipping time, the guides stretching from one side of the garden perimeter to the other, along the inside and outside edge of the hedges. However, once the hedge is at its established height and width, it should become easier to discern the growth to be pruned away without guides.

Yew (*Taxus baccata*) also responds to regular feeding, especially when newly planted. A high-nitrogen feed in early spring, followed by a general balanced fertilizer applied in midsummer, will guarantee active and healthy growth of at least 12 in. (30 cm) a year. Yew is unquestionably the finest evergreen hedging material, yet it has a reputation for slow growth. That and the high cost of large plants discourage many gardeners from using it, opting instead for the fast-growing and cheap Lawson cypress (x *Cupressus lawsoniana*). However, it is not always advisable to go for size when planting; new hedges establish more quickly if small young plants are used and yew, if fed as described, will soon make an effective hedge that is well worth the extra effort.

Yew is also a good choice for topiary work, like the cones shown here at the entrance to the parterre garden. Their shape picks up that of the trelliswork obelisks at the center of each box-edged corner bed, and over the top of the beech hedge can be seen repeated elsewhere in the garden. Well-defined vertical shapes and equally pronounced horizontals really come into their own in autumn when other parts of the garden are losing their definition.

The shrub border on the other side of the beech hedge from the parterre is studded with evergreens; *Euphorbia characias* ssp. *wulfenii*, *Choisya ternata*, *Viburnum davidii*, and a specimen yew like *Taxus baccata adpressa* offer interest in this border when the deciduous shrubs and herbaceous material have retired. The color

A mixed shrub border in late autumn includes plants chosen for their good stem structure, evergreen leaves, and inclination to carry faded flower or seedheads well into the first frosts of winter: I *Viburnum opulus* "Aureum"; II *Euonymus japonicus* "Aureopictus"; III *Sarcocca confusa*; IV *Magnolia stellata* "Waterlily"; V *Viburnum davidii*; VI *Viburnum sargentii* "Onondaga"; VII *Euphorbia characias*; VIII *Hebe* "Autumn Glory"; IX *Rosa moyesii* "Geranium"; X *Choisya ternata*; XI *Geranium endressii*; XII *Salvia officinalis*; XIII × *Heucherella tiarelloides*; XIV *Heuchera* "Palace Purple."

Left. The formal plan of the garden complements the architecture of the house. It also helps to sustain interest in the garden through long winter months, as do the desiccated flowers, evergreen groundcovers, and the contorted lines of naked branches in flower borders (*top*) and the frost-rimmed foliage of individual plants (*above*).

of the beech-hedge background lends depth and contrast to the evergreen shrubs, allowing them to show off their individual outlines and at the same time giving character to the frosted branches of neighboring shrubs.

Viburnums are good-value plants for winter gardens. *Viburnum davidii* makes a low spreading mound with deeply veined, dull green leaves that are buff-colored on the reverse; it has autumn clusters of shiny blue-black berries. *V. rhytidophyllum*, also evergreen, is upright-growing and in time makes a tall, spreading shrub hung with dull, heavily textured leaves. In the depths of winter it can look very sorry for itself so should really be kept for woodland planting rather than put into borders. The deciduous viburnums

color well in autumn, taking on dusky purple and pink tints in the leaves. One of the finest is *V. plicatum* "Mariesii," with horizontally spreading branches. The snowy-white flower corymbs float along their upper surface in early summer with the leaves hanging gracefully below each flower cluster; in autumn the leaves turn coppery purple. The ever-popular *V. bodnantense* "Dawn" colors prettily in autumn, then carries clusters of baby pink, sweetly scented flowers on naked branches throughout winter. For prolonged foliage interest there are some colored-leaf varieties, of which the best-known are *V. sargentii* "Onondaga," which is upright-growing with purple tinted foliage, and *V. opulus* "Aureum," with yellow leaves. Both of these should be grown in semi-shade.

A late summer border

Alan Gray's planting of a late-summer border at the Old Vicarage in east Norfolk, England, makes the utmost use of clump-forming grasses such as pennisetum, miscanthus, and pampas to create a leafy matrix for a limited palette of late-summer flowering perennials. Where most flower-dependent borders would have been cut down and tidied up before winter the grasses remain, along with some of the stiffer-stemmed perennials, to prolong the display in this part of the large formal gardens. So successful is this scheme that the border retains its beauty until the grasses are cut down the following spring, thus doubling its function by becoming a winter border as well.

At that time of year the grasses have faded to a soft biscuit beige, and combine well with ghostly silver shrubs like artemisia and lavender. The surviving branches of *Aster lateriflorus* form well-defined masses, as do clumps of dried flower stems from the various sedums. Among the billowing grasses, the upright sword-like leaves of *Phormium tenax* "Purpureum" create a strong visual rhythm.

Earlier in the year the green grasses make a fine foil for the shocking pinks and purples of neighboring flowering plants; in the background there are fronds of dark purple buddleia, *Buddleia davidii* "Black Knight," complemented by bright yellow broom *Genista lydia*; in the middleground there are roses, *Anemone japonica*, *Fuchsia magellanica* var. *gracilis* "Tricolor," and a number of Michaelmas daisies; the foreground is composed of sedums including *Sedum* "Ruby Glow" and *S.* "Vera Jameson," flushed deep cherry pink. *Schizostylis coccinea* scatters its cochineal-colored flowers amidst the silvers and rusts of its companions, which include *Artemisia ludoviciana* "Silver Queen," *A.* "Powis Castle," and patches of felted gray lamb's ears (*Stachys byzantina*). The warm pinks and violets of these flower colors are concentrated in the purple-bronze foliage of the phormium and *Heuchera* "Palace Purple," and also help to draw attention to the delicate coloring of the grass flowers.

Pennisetum alopecuroides is probably the most beautiful of the fountain grasses; the cascading leaves make a fine soft mound, above which the dusty pink flowers dangle like furry caterpillars caught on a line. *P. a.* "Hameln" is a lower-growing variety and *P. villosum* has the longest bristles for an even softer effect in the border. The flower plumes of the *Miscanthus* cultivars have a similar rosy glow, but their reflective texture gives them a silken shimmer. Grasses are monocots, fertilized by

This splendid border has everything you could ask for: color, texture, movement, myriad contrasts in height, and depth of tone; all is provided by the foundation of mixed grasses and strong foliage plants artfully composed with carefully blended flower color.

wind rather than insects, so that the flowers need only be composed of pollen-producing and pollen-receiving parts. Their simple structure enhances their allure as well as their longevity, but can mean that the flowers fade into insignificance. Yet when grasses are used as they are here, to form the foundation of a herbaceous border with the accompanying flower colors used as accents, the usually muted grass flowers sing out.

Miscanthus species and in particular cultivars of *Miscanthus sinensis*, the eulalia grass, are used through the border to provide the bulk of the leafy matrix. *M. sinensis* offers the gardener a huge range of cultivars to choose from for height, shape, spread, and flower effect. Among the other popular miscanthus species, *M. sacchariflorus* gives the most dramatic show. It is similar in appearance to *Arundo donax* but somewhat hardier, although in zones where the temperature falls to 41° F (-5° C) it is wise to mulch the base of the plant; any colder than that and it would be safest to lift it and overwinter under glass.

Miscanthus sacchariflorus is rhizomatous; *M. sinensis*, on the other hand, is clump-forming and offers a large selection of tall-growing grasses. Some of these have striking variegation, like the white-edged cultivars *M. sinensis* "Morning Light" and *M. s.* "Variegatus," or *M. s.* "Zebrinus," which carries its yellow stripes across the width of each leaf. *M. s.* "Kascade" has long, pendulous flower plumes; *M. s.* "Rotsilber" has silvery-pink plumes and *M. s.* "Malepartus" has burgundy-colored plumes that fade to silver. *M. s.* "Flamingo" has good russet autumn foliage and *M. s.* "Gracillimus" has the narrowest foliage, curling at the tips.

It is often recommended that miscanthus be grown in regal isolation as specimen plants, and it is true that they do need room to expand to their full beauty and should never be so crowded that their natural habit is impaired. However, by choosing neighbors carefully for the contrast they offer the graceful falling curve of the foliage can be accentuated and, as seen in the Old Vicarage border here, the subtle color of the flower plumes enhanced. Certainly, the spiky leaves of the *Phormium tenax* serve both purposes in Alan's planting.

While the scheme of this border tends to follow the formal tradition of positioning tall subjects at the back and keeping ground-huggers to the front, there is an occasional surprising juxtaposition, as with the tall-growing *M. sacchariflorus* planted quite boldly in the foreground. Touches like this save a border in which plant groups are uniformly repeated from monotony.

In late autumn and winter the light is lower and soft colors can be lost on gray days. It helps to take this into account when choosing the site for a seasonally dedicated border like this, and try to position it so that the plant foliage is caught in the low-angled light of the morning and evening sun. This is particularly worth attention when trying to make the most of the grass flow-

ers; even the more obvious plumes of *Cortaderia selloana* "Pumila" rise above the commonplace when spotlit by a low-slanted sunbeam. This is the dwarf pampas grass, best suited to border cultivation. It is probably the most freely flowering cultivar, but there are several other excellent ones to choose between. Pampas grass is often planted in the middle of a lawn, given solitary confinement in a circular bed — a throwback to the days of the Victorian garden when big plant equaled specimen plant. If this appeals to you go for *C. s.* "Sunningdale Silver," which is a large-flowered form with the plumes held well above the mound of grassy foliage. The stems are particularly sturdy and are most able to resist strong wind; too often the appearance of a specimen pampas grass is spoiled by the litter of broken flower stems.

For the border, however, there are some magnificent cultivars. *Cortaderia selloana* "Violacea," for example, has striking flower panicles strongly violet tinted — hence the name. *C. s.* "Aureolineata," sometimes called "Gold Band," is a real eye-catcher, with each leaf edged in a broad band of yellow that gradually takes over, turning the leaves solid gold with age. It has attractive flower plumes as well.

Apart from the phormium, the other dark tones are provided by the red-leaved sedums mentioned above and the coral bell cultivar *Heuchera* "Palace Purple." This cultivar has been popular for a very long time, but a new generation bred by American growers is coming on to the market. These plants have larger leaves, taller flower stalks, more strikingly variegated foliage,

Above. A planting plan of the Old Vicarage late summer border: I *Genista* x *spachiana*; II *Eucalyptus*; III *Cortaderia selloana* "Pumila"; IV *Buddleia* "Black Knight"; V *Miscanthus sacchariflorus*; VI *Aster pilosus* var. *demotus*; VII *Aster lateriflorus* "Horizontalis"; VIII *Rosa mutabilis*; IX *Miscanthus* "Silberfeder"; X *Fuchsia magellanica* "Variegata"; XI *Phormium tenax* "Atropurpureum"; XII *Miscanthus* "Morning Light"; XIII *Aster × frikartii* "Mönch"; XIV Artemisia *"Powis Castle"*; XV *Artemisia ludoviciana*; XVI *Artemisia densum*; XVII *Heuchera* "Palace Purple"; XVIII *Pennisetum alopecuroides*; XIX *Schizostylus coccineus*; XX *Ajania pacifica*; XXI *Sedum spectabile*; XXII *Helichrysum italicum.*

and increased hardiness. Among the new cultivars I look forward to growing are *H.* "Chocolate Ruffles" with deeply lobed, wavy-edged leaves that are chocolate brown above and bright purple on the reverse, *H.* "Plum Pudding," a rich vinous purple, and *H.* "Purple Petticoats," a dark purple with crimped edges.

Above is a small and simple scheme for a "nibble-sized" piece of edible landscaping. The plants used are: I Squash; II Sweetcorn; III Lettuce "Lollo Rosso"; IV Box hedge; V Purple-podded climbing French bean; VI Ruby chard; VII Runner bean; VIII Silver beet chard.
Left Villandry's monumental potager, of which a small portion is shown here, is composed with seemingly militaristic discipline — there's not an ornamental cabbage out of line. Each of the nine separate 100 ft. (30 m) squares is divided into its own unique pattern. Such grandeur can, however, inspire more homely designs, like the potager garden at The Old Rectory in Northamptonshire, England (*opposite*). Here, leaf beet, silver chard, sweet-corn, runner bean flowers, and crimson beetroots are mustered to create an aesthetically pleasing but functional garden.

Edible landscaping

Don't ever underestimate the value of vegetables in garden design. We are all familiar with the beauty of a carefully plotted potager, where the shape and color of each vegetable variety is as important for what it contributes to the design of the garden as its value to the cook, but such pretty plants don't have to be confined to the kitchen garden — they can contribute to the ornamental borders and shrubberies as well.

The most renowned potager is undeniably at the Château de Villandry in France, where, I've been told, the crop rotation is determined by a sophisticated computer program. Clearly, the programmer has excellent taste as well, for the skillfully manicured beds are filled each year with vegetable combinations that thoughtfully contrast leaf shape, texture, plant form, and color. In the photograph illustrated, blocks of blue-green, ribbon-leaved leeks contrast with squares of white-stemmed, fan-leaved Swiss chard; bands of white and purple-centered ornamental cabbage frame the quarters, and borders of tomatoes are studded with radiant orange fruit.

When many of the vegetables grown in Europe today were first introduced from the Americas, they were grown as garden, and even personal, decoration; the fine feathery foliage of carrot tops was used to decorate fashionable ladies' hats and scarlet runner beans were valued for their bright red flowers and grown as ornamental climbers.

Today, we have an enormous menu of edible ornamentals to choose from, gathered from all over the world. In the Orient, tender young hosta leaves and the variegated leaves of *Houttuynia cordata* are used in salads and as flavoring — the latter as a substitute for coriander leaf. Less exotically, there are the very colorful lettuce varieties like "Petite Rouge" and "Ibis," with frilled and crinkled leaves tinted varying shades of mahogany red, ruby chard with cardinal-red stems and veins supporting the emerald-green leaves, and red-stemmed rhubarb. There are purple brussels sprouts, leeks, French beans, peas, and even sweetcorn with purple-tinted foliage. Even the humble cabbage has its stars; "Rodeo" is a variety to look for. Think of the various fruits; yellow squashes, red, yellow, orange, and striped tomatoes, purple onions. To these you can add all the

gray-leaved herbal shrubs like sage and lavender (used to flavor refreshing sorbets and creams), gilded rosemary with yellow-splashed leaves, and architectural herbs and vegetables like bronze-leaved fennel, artichokes, and cardoons. Asparagus fronds are highly decorative and turn a rich golden green in autumn; female plants will have red berries. Variegated-leaf strawberries make bold bright edgings.

Most of the edibles will be annual crops, so potagers are often edged in box and the pathways permanently paved in order to provide structure in a part of the garden that would otherwise lack interest during all but the growing season. Permanent plantings of fruit and nut trees and bushes can be used to reinforce the design; apple trees can be trained into ornamental shapes and stepover edgings and hazelnuts can be shaped into living arbors. Use golden hops to cover fences and train ornamental gourds through trelliswork.

Regarding maintenance, there are the usual practicalities of vegetable-growing to deal with; pests and diseases don't change and observation of crop rotation to maintain soil fertility is just as important in a potager as in an ordinary vegetable plot. When lay-ing out the garden, make beds only as wide as is comfortable to reach to their middle without undue stretching or stepping on the bed. Paths should be wide enough to walk down comfortably while pushing a wheelbarrow, and corners must allow for easy maneu-vering of the barrow.

Obviously, if you are going to harvest the potager rather than just looking at it you will need to have back-up supplies of young plants to put into positions where a lettuce or cabbage is cut; root crops and others that cannot be renewed through the height of the season should be gathered evenly through the planting — in other words, don't pull a row of carrots, just take individuals here and there as though you were thinning.

Don't be in too big a hurry to cut down and tidy up at the end of the season; even a row of bolted red lettuce has a curious charm about it. Seedheads from umbelliferous plants (belonging to the carrot family) like fennel, lovage, and dill are extremely pretty, and red orach left to seed makes a tall spike covered in copper-brown seed discs. They'll scatter all over, but then you can have the plea-sure of self-sown seedlings the following year.

A container garden

Some of the most dramatic foliage plants are natives of subtropical regions and in order to use these plants in the garden most of us must grow them as pot plants. How I envy gardeners in Florida and Spain who are able to create entire gardens from plants I must nurture carefully on my windowsills and in the conservatory. Some of the most fantastic exotic landscapes are those created by the Brazilian artist and architect Roberto Burle Marx. He began to garden as a child, and during the eighteen months the family spent in Berlin, Burle Marx was able to study Brazil's native flora in the collections of the Dahlem Botanic Gardens, where he became determined to investigate the potential of this huge range of tropical plants for use in landscaping. Burle Marx was dismayed by the Brazilian tendency to ape the formalized gardens of France and Portugal; he saw how unsuitable the style and the plants used were for the Brazilian climate. Native plants, with their bold shapes, hugely varied textures, and rich colors allowed him to execute some of the twentieth century's finest landscapes, where a large part of their success lay in the fact that not only were the plants physically suited to the habitats but also aesthetically in tune, and able to hold their own in the dramatic extremes of weather, light, and climate.

Burle Marx's landscapes ranged from the 5 mile (8 km) long promenade along the beach at Copacabana to intimate courtyards, and in each he deftly manipulated the plant and hard landscaping to suit the scale of the project. Temperate gardens can imitate some of Burle Marx's boldness by incorporating exotic plants in so-called "tropical" borders where plants like the banana (*Musa bajoo*) can rub shoulders with canna lilies, and the multi-hued cultivars of the houseplant stalwart *Coleus blumei* can be elevated to Mardi Gras splendor in association with begonias, marantas, caladiums (which deserve to be more widely grown, in containers and "tropical" summer borders), and any number of tender foliage plants. All it takes is the nerve to liberate them from the windowsill.

If, however, you find the idea of transferring these plants to the herbaceous border rather unsettling, you could break yourself in gently by beginning with containers. Terracotta urns, lead (real or fake) water tanks, and wooden barrels can all offer exotics a safe temporary home in the temperate outdoors. When you plant exotic containers, you must do so with the same boldness and vitality that these showy plants express by their very nature. At Bourton House, near Chipping Campden in Gloucestershire, England, this concept has been taken to heart, and containers are carefully composed with a keen eye to suiting the shape, texture, and color of the plants to each other and to their mellow and very English setting. Flowers are used in moderation and generally tend to be long-lived, robust plants like fuchsia and the long lasting *Argyranthemum* "Jamaica Primrose."

The largest grouping is housed in an antique lead water tank, its soft matte gray surface texture echoed by the velvety foliage

An attractive container planted with a thoughtfully composed collection of foliage plants offers gardeners with even the smallest space the chance to grow exotic gems like this *Echeveria glauca* (*right*) or more extravagant jewel box displays of plectranthus, begonia, and silvery senecio (*left*) or even the distinctively architectural agaves (*opposite*).

Scale is an important consideration when planting containers and, in general, the bigger the better as a large pot or huge basket such as this allows for a wider range of more dramatic plants to be grown to make real impact.

of the many species of *Plectranthus* used as the foundation planting. *P. madagascariensis*, commonly called variegated mintleaf, takes the high point in the composition, with the broad felted leaves of *P. fruticosus*, *P. argentatus*, and dark-tinted *P. oertendahlii* below. To contrast with the rounded shapes of this foliage, *Senecio kleinia* is used for its succulent steel-blue fingers.

A small, shallow lead trough is planted for high contrast, with the rosette-forming succulent *Echeveria glauca* played off against the strappy leaves of the hardy perennial black "grass" *Ophiopogon planiscapus* "Nigrescens." High tonal contrasts feature again in the planting of the oak-leaved peppermint-scented *Pelargonium* "Chocolate Peppermint" with its purple black-centered furry leaves supporting the soft green and mottled cream *Fuchsia magellanica* var. *gracilis* "Variegata." The leaves and stems of the background plant, *Fuchsia* "Gartenmeister Bonstedt," repeat the inky color of the peppermint geranium.

Butter-yellow variegations mottle the huge round leaves of the perennial *Petasites japonicus* var. *giganteus* "Variegatus" which, with a white-edged hosta, set the color themes of a wall-mounted basket. The yellow is repeated in the delicate crown of daisy flowers of *Argyranthemum* "Jamaica Primrose" and the grassy leaves of gold-striped *Hakonechloa macra* "Alboaurea"; the trailing variegated mintleaf adds to the white variegations and purple-leaved *P. oertendahlii* and more of the dark-hearted "Chocolate Peppermint" pelargonium give tonal depth.

The plantings in each of the previously described containers are fairly complex, and their impact is heightened by the unifying repetition of certain plants. Yet there are also simple schemes that make use of only two plants, one for flower, the other for foliage, partnered for complementary effects, such as the lime-green trailing *Helichrysum petiolare* "Limelight" and burnt orange-flowers of *Begonia sutherlandii*.

One of the most magnificent exotic foliage plants for garden or container is *Agave americana*. At Bourton House the yellow-edged

Container-grown displays of foliage plants are more maintenance intensive than a garden border; plants must be watered regularly, fed routinely (with a foliar feed if possible), and groomed daily to remove faded leaves and flowers.

cultivar *A. a.* "Variegata" is planted with *Helichrysum petiolare* "Limelight" and the succulent *Echeveria harmsii*, which has yellow-lipped crimson flowers. *Agave americana* is colored blue-gray, and the saw-toothed leaves are fogged with a soft powdery bloom; apart from *A. a.* "Variegata," there are two other striped cultivars: *A. a.* "Marginata," with white variegation, and *A. a.* "Mediopicta," with yellow stripes down the center of each leaf.

In a grand assemblage at the entrance to the house, a number of pots are gathered together at the foot of a terracotta urn which is planted with the peppermint-scented geranium used elsewhere and three widely contrasting foliage plants: *Phormium tenax* with its tough strappy leaves; *Salvia confertiflora* with its oval leaves with a felted texture; and *Melianthus major*, barely visible behind the sage, which has segmented leaves colored a pleasing bloomy blue-gray. This really is a plant worth going out of your way for, unless the scent of the leaves, reminiscent of burnt chocolate, is not to your liking.

Showy displays like this really do make the most of the foliage of tender plants, but to maintain the eye-popping quality the plants must be tended daily. Most of these plants prefer well-drained soil and will grow in semi-shade. Remember that rainforest natives will want humidity and low light, while others, like agave, salvia, and melianthus, don't mind sun and parched conditions. Take the time to familiarize yourself with your plants' requirements. Other counsels of perfection are attention to watering, as some pots will have to be watered twice a day; sluice down the pot as well. Pinch out the growing tips of the plants to keep them in good shape and to encourage bushiness. One of the goals of container gardening with tender foliage plants is to maintain a full and healthy display over a much longer season than you could ever achieve with familiar hardy flowering plants, so feed the plants regularly as watering will leach out the nutrients in soil mixes; foliar feeds are especially good to use in this situation because they are formulated to meet the needs of leafy plants.

A hosta border

In early spring the gardens at Hadspen House in Somerset, England, resume their subtle color harmonies, and the hosta borders show how to make best use of this favorite foliage perennial.

Massed plantings of one genus can be quite awe-inspiring and that is certainly the case here, with dozens of different hosta cultivars used to edge a garden path. White-variegated forms mingle with yellow-variegated, and broad-leaved, glaucous-blue varieties contrast with narrow-leaved, acid-green ones. Hostas are at their peak in summer, but unlike many herbaceous perennials they contribute to the garden scene from the moment the foliage begins to unwrap itself until the final meltdown of the last faded leaf. Early in the season, before the plants unfurl their leaves, the space between them can be occupied by spring-flowering bulbs: at Hadspen, miniature daffodils and pure yellow tulips are used along with the yellow-variegated grass *Hakonechloa macra* "Alboaurea," planted in clumps towards the front of the border. The head of the path is framed by *Euphorbia characias, Nectaroscordum siculum* (a bulb in the allium family, with pendant, bell-shaped flowers colored white and flushed plum down the center of each petal), and bronze fennel *Foeniculum vulgare* "Purpureum." As the season progresses, the faded bulbs vanish beneath the shade of the spreading hosta leaves.

Hostas vary in color from glaucous blue to acid green and almost yellow, with variegations in assorted distributions — edgings, splashes, midrib streaks — and shades of white, cream, and yellow. One of the most popular is glaucous-blue *H.* "Frances Williams" with pale biscuity beige edges. *H.* "Blue Umbrellas," *H.* "Blue Angel," and the heavily textured *H.* "Love Pat" are among the best blue-grays. The series named for the garden have, in the case of *H.* "Hadspen Blue," *H.* "Hadspen Hawk," and *H.* "Hadspen Heron," glaucous-blue foliage, while *H.* "Hadspen Samphire" has yellow, lanceolate leaves. *H.* "Sum and Substance" has huge golden leaves, while *H.* "Sun Power" is one of the few yellow-leaved hostas that will tolerate a few hours of direct sun each day. *H.* "Shade Fanfare," *H.* "Wide Brim," and *H.* "Nancy Lindsay" all have yellow variegation. *H.* "Patriot" is one of the brightest white variegated hostas with large, heart-shaped leaves that are emerald green in the center and edged with broad borders of snowy white; *H.* "Frosted Jade," *H.* "Francee," and *H.* "Big Boy" also have large leaves with white variegation.

On the whole, hostas require a semi-shaded position in well-drained soil which does not dry out. Yellow-leaved and variegated hostas require more shade as the leaves tend to scorch in sun. Cool, moist conditions are particularly important in warmer climates, but in cooler regions hostas will tolerate dry (not arid) conditions helped by their fleshy roots.

The Hadspen gardens are made in an old walled vegetable garden situated on a gentle south-facing slope. To overcome the sun-drenched environment the Popes planted a hornbeam avenue and in autumn the hornbeam leaves fall on to the border, helping to maintain humus levels. In the summertime, when the sun scorches the surrounding borders, a stroll down the shady length of this leafy tunnel provides the garden visitor with welcome and refreshing respite.

The hosta border at Hadspen House is part of the long, double borders (*opposite*) devoted to plants with yellow leaves and flowers. The cultivars suggested in this plan would produce a similar effect: I *Euphorbia characias*; II *Hosta* "Gold Standard"; III *Hosta* "Sum and Substance"; IV *Tulipa* "Yellow Purissima" (Fosteriana hybrid); V *Hosta* "Aureomarginata"; VI *Hosta* "Green Gold"; VII *Hosta* "Royal Standard"; VIII *Hosta* "Frances Williams"; IX *Hosta* "Kabitan"; X *Hosta* "Phyllis Campbell"; XI *Hosta* "Albo-picta"; XII *Hosta* "Aureomaculata"; XIII *Hakonechloa* "Alboaurea" XIV *Hosta sieboldii* "Alba."

A bog garden

Foliage plants and water features are an especially attractive combination. The still surface of a garden pond will mirror the shapes and textures of overhanging foliage, thereby enhancing the effect of a well-planted bog garden.

A bog garden is one in which the soil is permanently wet, and a boggy area is usually included in the construction of modern artificial garden ponds by lowering one edge of the pond so that water seeps into a specially prepared trench running alongside it. The pond liner fabric needs to be large enough to overlap the trench, and while care must be taken not to puncture the actual pond area of the liner, holes are poked through the part of the liner that will be underneath the bog garden soil mix, which contains plenty of moisture-holding humus or peat. The same effect can be achieved when making a formal pool.

One of the most magnificent of all the marginal plants to grow at the water's edge is *Gunnera manicata*, and in the garden at Hadspen House a single plant sets the stage for a composition which makes the most of contrasts in size. The leaves of a mature gunnera can reach 5 ft. (1.5 m) across, while a plant grown in optimum conditions will easily make 8 ft. (2.5 m) — finding shelter beneath one on a rainy day can give you the distinct impression of being in a tropical jungle. The vast lobed leaves have a bristly surface, as does the thick stalk; the flowers form at the heart of the plant and look like giant pine cones. *G. tinctoria* has more rounded leaves with shorter stalks, but will still give substance to a bog-garden planting scheme.

Gunneras like sun as well as deep moist soil, and although they are fairly hardy it is a good idea to give the resting crowns protection in winter; when the leaves fade, fold them inwards to cover the crown, apply a thick blanket of well-rotted manure or soil mix, and cover with bracken if you live in an area in which winters are particularly severe.

Rodgersias also offer some excellent foliage plants and *Rodgersia pinnata* "Superba" is probably the finest, with segmented, heavily textured leaves that are tinted rich mahogany purple. It grows to about 3 ft. (90 cm) in height from creeping underground rhizomes, and will accept sun or semi-shade, but must have cool moisture at the roots. Similarly, *R. podophylla* has segmented leaves, each leaflet being roughly triangular in shape with serrated edges. Young leaves have a rich chocolatey tint, fading to green for summer and resuming a brownish tinge as they mature.

Darmera peltata, formerly known as *Peltiphyllum peltatum*, has round, crinkly leaves with scalloped edges, about 12 in. (30 cm) across, that are held aloft to about 2 ft. (60 cm) on thick stems. The naked flower stems make a curious sight, rising like

a fakir's snakes above the leafy mound. It will gradually colonize a bog garden by creeping rhizomatous roots, but can be controlled by ripping out chunks as necessary. *D. p.* "Nana," as you might expect, is a smaller version with purple-tinted leaves that are closer to the ground, reaching to about 8 in. (20 cm).

With all these broad rounded shapes, it is a good idea to add a counterpoint by the use of a single contrasting shape, as provided here by narrow-leaved plants like *Carex elata* "Aurea" and *Iris sibirica* "Snow Queen." *Miscanthus sinensis* "Variegatus" is another narrow-leaved plant which provides bright contrast. It is one of the oldest cultivars of miscanthus and carries its white-striped leaves in loose clumps. In autumn the foliage pales to an attractive almond color. It is surprisingly shade tolerant and in hot climates should be planted in light shade to prevent leaf burn. One often sees gardener's garters (*Phalaris arundinacea* var. *picta*) used in or near bog gardens; a better common name would be "gardener's torment" for its invasive nature can be just that. The cultivar *P. a.* var. *picta* "Feesey" is more brilliantly white, and supposedly less invasive.

Above. A planting scheme inspired by Hadspen includes: I *Gunnera manicata*; II *Darmera peltata*; III *Carex elata* "Aurea"; IV *Hosta sieboldiana*; V *Geranium* "Johnson's Blue"; VI *Iris sibirica* "Snow Queen."
Left. The whippy flower stems of *Darmera peltata* echo the linear foliage of *Carex elata* "Bowles Gold" and siberian iris, and contrast with the rounded shapes of the remaining foliage.

A woodland edge garden

The cool dappled shade to be found at the edge of a woodland provides excellent growing conditions for a wide range of shrubs and perennials that are valuable for their foliage as well as their flower color.

Anne Waring has utilized this fact in the marvelous leafy patchwork she has created in her West Sussex, England, garden "North Springs" by mingling a wide range of trees, shrubs, and perennials in an informal planting. The layered planting of the garden helps it to merge effortlessly into the woodland setting; the verticals of the surrounding trees are echoed in the garden by the upright shapes from a range of conifers. Other evergreens provide a permanent anchor for the island perennial beds: *Pieris japonica*, *Mahonia lomariifolia*, and *Berberis* cultivars all have strong forms, good foliage shape, and interesting textures. Deciduous shrubs, including variegated *Weigela praecox* "Variegata" and *Cornus mas*, with bright green leaves, or *C. m.* "Variegata," fill out the background planting. The spindleberry *Euonymus alatus* makes an attractive spreading shrub that takes on fiery autumn colors. Beneath this sheltering layer a path winds between clumps of hosta; by using variegated varieties and cultivars, as Anne has, you can introduce a

Above. A planting plan suggested by the woodland edge garden at North Springs includes: I *Angelica archangelica*; II *Polemonium caeruleum*; III *Hosta sieboldiana*; IV *Iris pseudacorus*; V *Lysichiton americanus*; VI *Ligularia dentata* "Desdemona"; VII *Senecio smithii*; VIII *Symphytum* 'Goldsmith'; IX *Filipendula ulmaria* 'Aurea'; X *Filipendula purpurea*; XI *Hosta crispula*; XII *Trollius* x *cultorum* 'Superbus'; XIII *Hosta undulata* var. *univittata*; XIV *Bergenia* "Bressingham White"; XV *Hosta* "Gold Standard"; XVI *Rodgersia pinnata*; XVII *Symphytum* x *uplandicum* "Variegatum"; XVIII *Lysimachia punctata*.
Opposite. The layered approach to planting the woodland garden at North Springs evokes a natural informality while simultaneously providing the right conditions for plants to flourish.

range of tints to which other foliage plants can be related. *Hosta undulata* var. *univittata* has bold white streaks that are repeated in the leaves of *Symphytum* × *uplandicum* "Variegatum" and *Astrantia major* "Sunningdale Variegated"; *Hosta* "Gold Standard" is splashed with yellow, as is *Symphytum* "Goldsmith," this color being emphasized by groundcovering plants like *Lysimachia nummularia* "Aurea" and glowing clumps of *Filipendula ulmaria* "Aurea."

Many broad-leaved perennials need moist conditions to perform well and to keep the foliage in good condition, especially if they in turn are expected to provide shade for groundcovers. *Rodgersia pinnata* and *Ligularia dentata* "Desdemona" provide good dense color in the garden with their vinous purple undersides, but both will droop dismally when the soil begins to dry out. Even more demanding are *Lysichiton americanus* (skunk cabbage), with glossy tapering leaves that appear long before the flower spathe, and *Senecio smithii*, which has the same high-gloss finish; both prefer to have their roots in water. The reflective surfaces of plants like these bring the brightness of indirect light into a shaded area; *Acanthus mollis* (bear's breeches) is another glossy-leaved perennial with particularly strong architectural foliage, a feature it shares with the herb *Angelica archangelica*.

A dry sunny garden

In complete contrast to the moist conditions found in a woodland garden, this garden enjoys freely draining soil and a sun-baked south-facing aspect. Sandwiched between the hills rising up behind the French village of Giverny and the Loire river, the garden occupies the site of the old vegetable garden. The house, next door to Monet's, was once occupied by Leila Cabot Perry, a patroness of the American Impressionists. The house and garden are undergoing restoration, with the garden project under the direction of the garden designer Mark Brown.

When restoring the flower garden area in front of the house, Brown studied the paintings of Frederick Carl Frieseke which show the garden as it was when Mrs. Cabot Perry was in residence. There are rose borders and many colorful annuals; the lawn is studded with dwarf apple trees and edged by a perennial border and step-

over apple hedge. Adjacent to this formal part of the garden there was a derelict kitchen garden which received a very different treatment. Its entirely new design and planting reflects Brown's abiding interest in naturally occurring plant *biomes*, the term used in France to express the idea of grouping plants according to their ability to accept the same soil and light conditions. Taking his lead from the flora of the hills above the village, Brown has created a garden of grasses and herbs suited to a sun-filled site. The ground

is warm and well-drained and ideal for the sages, verbascums, catmints, marjorams, thymes, and other perennial herbs woven into the grassy matrix of blue-green *Sesleria caerulea* in the center of the garden and *Brachypodium distachyon* in the perimeter areas.

There are gardeners who disregard the potential of grasses, seeing them only as a voguish plant which will eventually be surpassed by another as garden fashion changes. However, with ecology and conservation high on the agenda, the horticultural world is increasingly concerned with establishing energy-efficient gardens which are compatible with existing conditions. It must be acknowledged that there are few plants as adaptable to a variety of moods and settings as grass, and also few that will provide such a varied and pleasing display over such a long season. From early spring when fresh green shoots begin to emerge through summer flowering and seed-forming to late autumn when burnished reds and browns replace the verdant green, ornamental grasses mark the changes of season like no other herbaceous plant.

Apart from the sesleria and brachypodium which are the foundation planting of the garden, there are a number of other showy grasses given prominence, including clumps of feather-fine *Stipa tenuissima* and its splendid relation *S. gigantea*. Stipas are among the most graceful grasses in the garden: early in the season *S. tenuissima* holds itself erect, but as the fine silky seedheads begin to form it droops to make a filmy mound of warm golden tints. *S. gigantea*, however, sends up erect flowers stems to about 2 ft. (60 cm) from which dangle the large oat-shaped seedheads that glitter and bob in the lightest breeze. Both plants are easy to propagate from seed; with *S. tenuissima* you simply comb out the filamented seedheads and spread the mass evenly on the surface of a trayful of soil mix. Sieve a thin layer of soil mix over the top, water gently, and leave to germinate in a semi-shaded spot. Prick out in small clumps into separate pots or line out in nursery beds. *S. gigantea* seeds can be handled individually by the long corkscrew-twisted filament and sown in trays. Another graceful oat-type grass in the garden is *Chasmanthium latifolium*, a native of North America much loved for its graceful dangling panicles of broad flat seeds that stir in the slightest breeze.

Bamboos are also featured in the garden to shade a seating area at one end of a wisteria-covered pergola and at the furthest end of the garden to make a shelter belt which serves as a noise baffle, cutting the intrusive decibels generated by the busy main road beyond the garden walls. Apart from its graceful habit, bamboo has music and movement — from the sound and sway of its leaves and canes stirring in the breeze — and mystery; a bamboo grove creates a

Mark Brown drew inspiration from the south-facing slopes of the hills behind Giverny to create this tranquil oasis of herbs and grasses. In late summer when the herbs bloom, the garden drifts in a soft blue sea of flower color enhanced by the blue-gray foliage that predominates.

shadowy mass through which bright sun can only trickle. The canes of some cultivars and species of the genus *Phyllostachys* have the most subtle colorings, from the dark, cocoa-brown of mature *P. nigra* to the sunny yellow of *P. aurea* "Holochrysa." There are variegated stem colorings too: *P. vivax* "Aureocaulis" has green and yellow markings, while *P. nigra* "Boryana" is blotched with brown. *P. flexuosa* is the Chinese weeping bamboo, with dark purple canes; it needs plenty of space.

As autumn arrives the grasses become a warm tint of honey gold enameled with the cobalt-blue flowers of *Catananche caerula, Nepeta* "Six Hills Giant," *Perovskia atriplicifolia,* and numerous other hillside herbs, which then leave behind the burnished umbels, panicles, and pods that are full of next year's promise.

Left. The angel-hair delicacy of *Stipa tenuissima* is in pointed contrast to the agressive shape of the wild thistle growing in its midst.
Opposite. The texture of the erect stems of hyssop, lychnis, perovskia, and *Stipa gigantea* blend together, but the plants form distinct layers of color.
Below. Dry gardens and gravel paths lend themselves to this kind of natural habitat-influenced gardening. Plants used are: I *Paeonia lactiflora* "White Wings"; II *Nepeta x faassenii*; III *Catananche caerulea* "Major"; IV *Sesleria caerula*; V *Stipa gigantea*; VI *Salvia pratensis*; VII *Helianthemum* "The Bride"; VIII *Verbascum nigrum*; IX *Stipa tenuissima*; X *Cynoglossum nervosum*; XI *Echinops ritro*; XII *Brachypodium distachyon*; XIII *Asphodelus albus.*

A late season shrub garden

A friend of mine who lives in Boston sent me a photograph of her winter garden. All one could make out were lumpy white shapes like toppled snowmen, hinting that there was indeed something under all that snow. It might have been a shrub, or it could have been a garbage can. When conditions are that extreme, there is little to do but long for the thaw, but Sally's reminder of what gardening can be like did make me appreciate anew how the color of bark on various trees and shrubs can brighten a garden in even the most remorseless winter.

There are certain shrubs that leap instantly to mind which are dependably hardy (even under a frosty shroud) and at the top of the list are the colored-stem dogwoods. *Cornus alba* "Argenteo-Marginata" has bright crimson stems and the added summer feature of variegated foliage; *C. a.* "Sibirica" has ruby-red stems; and *C. a.* "Kesselringii" has purplish-black stems. *C. a.* "Spaethii" and *C. a.* "Westonbirt" can also be relied upon to color well in leaf and stem, as can *C. a.* "Aurea," which has buttery-yellow autumn foliage on dark red stems. One other species worth noting is *C. stolonifera* "Flaviramea" which has egg-yolk yellow stems.

Other popular shrubs are the scarlet willow (*Salix daphnoides*) and the yellow willow (*S. alba vitallina*). Even the weeping willow (*S.* "Chrysocoma") has the most delicate yellow tint on its new growth. The violet willow (*Salix alba vitellina* "Britzensis") has a soft silvery bloom that turns the purple bark nearly white. Another shrub with a curious sheen on its stems is *Elaeagnus commutata*, which looks as though it has been dusted over with gold. Combined with leathery silver-gray leaves it makes quite a show, as does its relative *E. angustifolia*, which has delightful coppery fruit in dense clusters along the stems and long tapering gray leaves.

There are a few other good bright whites for shrub stem color and among the best are two silver-stemmed brambles, *Rubus cockburnianus* and *R. thibetanus*; the first is a much stronger white, but the latter's cultivar *R. t.* "Silver Fern" has particularly pretty foliage perfectly described by the name. The Japanese wineberry (*R. phoenicolasius*) has crimson stems densely covered in prickly little thorns; the undersides of the leaves are nicely silvered, so the plant is attractive for much of the year.

Using this collection of shrubs as a point of departure, and drawing inspiration from the gardens scenes shown here, I can imagine planting a winter corner that would be set alight by the low slanting sun of that season.

Most of the shrubs grow to about 5 ft. (1.2 m) so I would include a tree or two for height, probably the spectral white birch *Betula jacquemontii* "Jermyns." The best effect is had by growing it as a multi-stemmed specimen. However, if that would be too startling, the soft red bark of *Acer pensylvanicum* "Erythrocladum" could provide a warming glow. *Acer griseum* is the paperbark maple, and its peeling bark has an equally warm cinnamon tint.

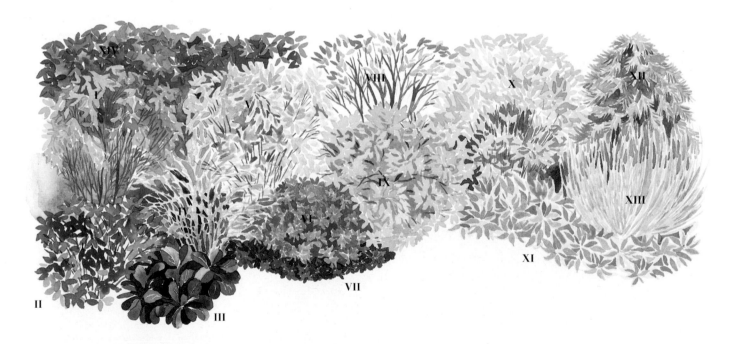

Opposite. Massed plantings of dogwood cultivars make a vibrant and demanding frame filled with perennials chosen for their leaf textures and harmonizing color. The plants suggested in the plan *(above)* are: I *Cornus alba* "Westonbirt"; II *Cornus florida* "Rainbow"; III *Bergenia crassifolia*; IV *Rubus biflorus*; V *Cornus alba* "Spaethii"; VI *Hebe pinguifolia* "Pagei"; VII *Ajuga reptans* "Purpurea"; VIII *Rubus phoenicolasus*; IX *Hamamelis × intermedia* "Jelena"; X *Cornus alba* "Aurea"; XI *Symphytum x uplandicum* "Variegatum"; XII *Chamaecyparis lawsoniana* "Winston Churchill"; XIII *Cornus stolonifera* "Flaviramea"; XIV *Parthenocissus tricuspidata*.

Left. Acer rubrum foliage brings a bold splash of color to autumn plantings. *Right.* There are many groundcovers, like *Bergenia crassifolia*, that color well. *Opposite.* Evergreens add depth to a predominantly deciduous group of trees.

There are any number of winter-coloring groundcovers to lay beneath the shrubs and one of the darkest is *Ajuga reptans* "Atropurpurea," which remains solidly purple through every kind of weather. *Parthenocissus tricuspidata* becomes a glossy flame-red mantle to spread on the ground or to throw over a wall. Other groundcovers could include *Nandina domestica* "Wood's Dwarf," a semi-evergreen (or rather ever-brown) dwarf shrub commonly called the sacred bamboo which would appreciate the shelter of the taller-growing shrubs.

Using an evergreen or two would give depth to the planting; perhaps *Chamaecyparis lawsoniana* "Winston Churchill," as shown here, or, if less of an exclamation mark is needed — merely a full stop — the tidy little *Cryptomeria japonica* "Globosa Nana." Bright shrubs with a touch of gold would bring the image of dappled light and shade and so give depth to the collection of stem and branch; either one of the hollies, perhaps *Ilex aquifolium* "Bacciflava," with its yellow berries, another elaeagnus, *Elaeagnus pungens* "Maculata," or, as groundcover, *Euonymus fortunei* "Emerald 'n' Gold."

Including a winter-flowering shrub, particularly in a walled garden where the scent would be less likely to blow away on the breeze, would add another layer of interest. For my money I would

include a witch hazel, such as *Hamamelis × intermedia* "Jelena" shown here. It is an orange-flowered cultivar of the familiar yellow-flowered species, with which it shares the same ethereal perfume. Witch hazel has pleasing autumn leaf colors, and a member of the same *Hamamelidaceae* family, *Disanthus cercidifolius*, has foliage that colors crimson and wine-red in autumn.

Colorfully stemmed plants need help to remain so, and the way to do this is to prune away the old growth to encourage new stems, since it is the new growth that has the best color. The ideal time to do this is in the early spring, just as the sap begins to rise. That way you will have enjoyed the colorful stems all autumn and winter, and will be setting the stage for the next season's display.

Some people recommend "stooling" which means removing absolutely every stick to leave behind a cluster of five or so stumps from which new growth will shoot. If the shrubs play an important structural role in the garden you may not want to remove so much, so the best thing to do is to remove only about one-third of the branches, beginning with the oldest wood. This is easy to recognize as it will have the darkest color and form the thickest branches in the shrub. (You may have to use a good pruning saw or parrot-nose shears rather than pruners.) Then remove any other growth that is damaged or tangled to leave a neat, open shape.

Right. Be bold with foliage plants in a small garden: you will find the dramatic effects and air of repose they create far more satisfying — and longer-lasting — than you could expect from a collection of plants chosen for their flower color alone.

Below. A narrow path beneath a canopy of evergreen and brightly colored foliage is edged with a variety of shade-loving shrubs, gold-variegated grasses like *Cortaderia selloana* "Sunstripe" and *Hakonechloa macra* "Alboaurea" and ground-covering ivies and tolmeia.

A courtyard garden

Sonny Garcia's small garden in northern California makes the most of its space by an abundant use of foliage. There are more than 150 different plants ranging from Chusan palms (*Trachycarpus fortunei*) to ground-covering *Tolmiea menziesii* "Taff's Gold," but even with this widely varying display, the leafy theme ensures that there is a feeling of quiet repose. The layers of planting, with their individual themes of contrast in leaf form and color, create their own rhythms. Drifts of grasses like the variegated *Cortaderia selloana* "Sunstripe" and *Hakeonechloa macra* "Alboaurea" skirt the edges of the paved paths, softening the hard edges with rounded shapes created by the mass of arching leaves.

Grasses add a sort of music to the garden, rustling like silken skirts disturbed by a passing breeze. This gentle sound enhances even further the tranquility of the garden and makes a satisfying substitute for water, a favorite "musical" accessory in garden design. Bamboo has a similar sound effect and could be used to make an effective screen, or to create a shady shelter belt beneath which contrasting low spreading shapes could be effectively brought into play. *Phyllostachys nigra* grows to only 12 ft. (3.5 m), with bright green young stems aging to black; using this to create strong verticals and contrasting its narrow ribbon leaves with the feathery fronds of *Aruncus dioicus* with a groundcover of a broad-leaved plant like hosta, perhaps the variegated *H. undulata* var. *univittata* would make a soothing garden corner.

In this garden, most of the larger shrubs have the most striking foliage as though to emphasize their importance as screens and backdrops to the groupings of lower-growing shrubs and herba-

Below. A planting plan that incorporates many of Sonny Garcia's design principles. I *Prunus cerasifera pissardii*; II *Cyathea cooperi*; III *Hakenechloa macra*; IV *Cordyline australis* "Albertii"; V *Acer pseudoplatanus* "Prinz Handjery"; VI *Cortaderia selloana* "Sunstripe"; VII Rhododendron; VIII Magnolia; IX Chusan palm (*Trachycarpus fortunei*); X *Lonicera nitida* "Baggesen's Gold"; XI *Spiraea japonica* "Goldflame"; XII *Cotinus coggygria*; XIII Apple espalier.

ceous plants with more subtle characters. There are rhododendrons with variegated leaves (always a good choice, since most plants within this group leave a boring dull green gap in a planting once their springtime flower show is over). There is also a *Magnolia* × *soulangeana*; unlike the evergreen rhododendrons, it sheds its leaves, which reappear after the spring flush of pink-tinted flowers. Their broad heavy nature combines well to make a shady enclave.

The shrubs seem to carry the color message with tints of bronze-purple and yellow being the main theme. *Acer palmatum* "Atropurpureum," *Prunus cerasifera* "Pissardii," *Cotinus coggygria* "Royal Purple," and *Phormium* "Dark Delight" are the most predominantly dark tinted foliage plants. There are a number of yellow variegated plants scattered throughout, with *Cortaderia selloana* "Sunstripe" and *Cordyline australis* "Albertii" bursting like sunspots through the clouds of foliage. *Lonicera nitida* "Baggesen's Gold" and

Spiraea japonica "Goldflame" are common yellow-leaved shrubs; more unusual is *Acer psuedoplatanus* "Prinz Handjery," which has shrimp pink juvenile leaves that change to green as they age. With such a dense planting, the groundcover shrubs must be shade tolerant like the yellow variegated ivy *Hedera helix* "Golden Child," which also brings brightness to shady depths, and *Liatris spicata*.

In a garden of this size (roughly 35 x 50 ft./10 x 15 m) it is necessary to prune hard — but thoughtfully — on a regular basis, not just to keep the garden from being overwhelmed, but also to keep the plants in good health. Close planting encourages etiolated growth, when new leaves ands stems appear thin and drawn, and such growth is susceptible to disease. So pruning to control size will improve the condition of the new growth, which will be healthy and well-formed. This is particularly relevant to plants grown specifically for their foliage as new branches always carry the best leaves.

PROPAGATION

THE PRACTICAL SIDE OF GARDENING IS NEVER FAR AWAY from the aesthetic concerns of planning and planting. In the case of a garden that makes the utmost use of foliage and stem color in massed plantings, propagation will be a prime concern; if carpets of foliage are not the main objective you may still want to increase stocks of a choice plant in your collection, or renew plantings that are beginning to deteriorate with age. It is also satisfying to share your plants with fellow gardeners, and if you open your garden to visitors plant sales can bring in extra revenue allowing you to increase your range of plants with new purchases.

Plants fall into several categories and within those categories various methods of propagation suit certain plants better than others. Working on the principle that it is always best to understand the whys as well as the wherefores, I have included here a potted primer of seed, stem, and leaf physiology; I believe an understanding of theory always helps practice to succeed.

In late summer, the flower spikes of the marginal water plant *Pontaderia cordata* are protected by their cloaks of bright glossy foliage. It is one of the few blue-flowered aquatics and may be propagated by division in spring.

Annuals

There are two sorts of annual plants, hardy annuals and half-hardy annuals. Both complete their life cycle in one year but the former are grown from seed sown *in situ* in spring or early autumn and the latter are sown under glass in late winter or early spring, usually with heat to aid germination, and then planted outside when all danger of frost is past.

Biennials

These grow and produce leaves in the first season then flower and die in the next. Seed is usually sown in summer in prepared seedbeds, then the plants are put out in their flowering positions the following spring. They can also be reproduced vegetatively, through cuttings.

Perennials

These plants live for many years. They include herbaceous perennials (including bulbs, corms, and tubers) which have a permanent root system but soft top growth that dies back annually; evergreen woody perennials, which have a permanent root system supporting a permanent woody structure that retains the leaves in winter; and deciduous woody perennials, which have the permanent root system and woody structure, but lose their leaves in winter. Perennials are usually reproduced vegetatively, although growing from seed is possible.

Seeds

Reproducing plants from seeds contained within berries and other capsules is a plant's method of sexual reproduction; all other methods like cuttings and divisions are vegetative. If you want to be sure of obtaining new plants which are identical to the old, you should use one of the vegetative methods described. Pollination is random if left to birds and insects, but by mixing the pollen of different species or making a selection within a species of individuals possessed of particularly fine qualities you can create new hybrids or cultivars respectively.

Flower structure

Seed from all sorts of plants can be sown and germinated with varying degrees of success, but to have seed you must have flowers. In order to understand the process of seed development and germination, it helps to know a little about flower structure.

Most flowers are hermaphrodites, containing male and female reproductive parts; some plants have separate male and female flowers on the same plant, while other plants are strictly single sex, either male or female. To obtain seed from the latter, you must have one plant of each sex.

The main parts of a flower are the petals, which are usually brightly colored and have scent glands to attract insects to aid pollination. They are arranged in a corolla, or ring, and each petal will have lines or grooves called honey guides which will lead the insect into the flower.

At the base of the flower are the sepals, forming the calyx, which protects the juvenile flower bud. Inside the flower are the stamens, made up of the pollen-bearing anthers supported on filaments which hold the anthers in the best position to transfer pollen (the male reproductive cell) to insects or to be caught by a breeze; when the pollen is ripe, the anthers split open to release it. Stamens are the male reproductive organs and are held in the part of the flower called the androecium.

The female parts are located in the very heart of the flower. The stigma receives the ripe pollen and is often sticky and feathery to aid the transfer; the style is a tube through which the pollen travels from the stigma to the ovary, which contains one or more ovules (the female reproductive cells). At the base of the ovaries are nectaries which produce nectar to attract insects and birds. The seeds are formed in the receptacle, at the point where the stalk and flower meet.

Pollination

There are two kinds of pollination: cross-pollination, when the pollen from one plant pollinates another, and self-pollination, when a plant pollinates its own flowers. There are two methods of cross-pollination – insect (which includes birds, slugs, snails, or other living creatures that effect the transfer of pollen) and wind pollination. Plants which rely on insect pollination have large, brightly colored or scented flowers, or a combination of these features. The anthers are small, on short filaments, and produce small quantities of pollen. The individual pollen grains have spiky surfaces so that they attach easily to passing insects. The stigma is also small and held deep within the plant. Wind pollinators generally have small, inconspicuous flowers without scent or nectar, and the anthers are held aloft on long filaments where they dangle like tiny lanterns. They make a bigger quantity of large, light pollen grains which are easily caught by the large feathery anthers that protrude outside the body of the flower.

Fertilization

Fertilization is the fusion of the pollen grain (male gamete) and the ovule (female gamete) when the pollen grain lands on the stigma (Fig. 5). Each gamete contains half the genetic information. Chemicals on the stigma will recognize whether or not the pollen is acceptable, thus preventing unsuitable cross-pollination between plant types. The pattern of the pollen must also match the pattern on the stigma to ensure the two will marry. Finally, there must be moisture.

If these conditions are met, the pollen produces a tube which grows down the style, absorbing nutrients as it goes, until it reaches the ovary where it penetrates an ovule at the micropyle, a small hole in the ovule. When that process is successfully completed, a pollen grain is released and moves down the tube into the ovule. There the male and female gametes fuse to form a zygote, an entire cell which starts to divide and ultimately become a seed (Fig. 5).

As soon as the flower is successfully fertilized it falls away or shrivels up, sometimes leaving the sepals behind. The developing zygote emits a hormone that induces the ovary to swell and become a fruit – either a fleshy berry or a dry, hard capsule. Brightly colored berries attract birds which then carry the seed in their gut, "sowing" it in their droppings around the garden; small animals take berries, nuts, and other dry seeds, and either bury them in caches or otherwise scatter the seed about the garden; and much dry seed is scattered by the wind.

Germination

If the conditions are right and the seed has been sown properly, germination takes place. The seed will begin to absorb moisture from the sowing medium through the micropyle and will grow either quickly if it is warm or slowly if cold (Fig. 6). It begins to absorb oxygen and this respiration breaks down the food reserves in the cotyledons, which also serve as the engines of photosynthesis before the first true leaves appear. The root bud, or radicle, elongates and breaks through the testa (the hard coat that protects the seed from diseases) at the micropyle. As the radicle grows it begins to produce lateral roots and root hairs that anchor the seedling and absorb nutrients. As it pushes

through the soil, the very tip of the radicle is protected by a tough little cap.

The hypocotyl, or vestigial stem, then begins to lengthen, which has the effect of pulling the cotyledons out of the soil (Fig. 6a). Up to this point the cotyledons have been protecting the plumule of first true leaves from damage but as the plumule increases in size the cotyledons split apart, allowing the leaves to expand on the developing shoot as the hypocotyl continues to lengthen and straighten up from its swan-necked posture (Fig. 7). This is the process of germination for dicotyledons (dicots), or plants that have two cotyledons.

Monocotyledons (monocots) – plants with one cotyledon – germinate rather differently (Fig. 8). The radicle and the plumule are contained within a sheath called the coleorhiza. The radicle breaks through this and the testa first, then the plumule emerges, wrapped in its coleophile sheath. This sheath splits and the first true leaves emerge.

Most plants are dicots, and in these the cotyledons protrude above the soil to begin photosynthesis. The leaves have a midrib and secondary veins arranged in branched networks. The stem is formed from tidy concentric rings of vascular tissue composed of phloem, xylem, and cambium (Fig. 9), and there is usually only one true root system, although secondary or adventitious roots are formed by some plants along the stems above ground, allowing the plant to root where it touches the soil and so take in extra nutrients to support more growth. The flowers consist of petals and sepals produced in fours and fives.

Monocot plants have a single cotyledon that is usually left beneath the soil. The leaves are simple single shapes, usually long and tapering, and with parallel veins running the length of the leaf. The vascular bundles are scattered throughout the stem, which is often quite spongy. Roots are fibrous, most often adven-

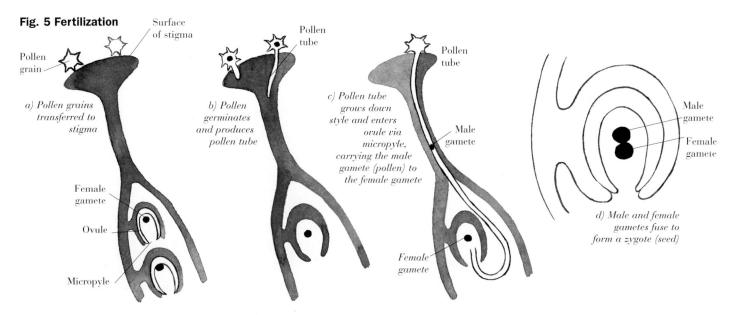

Fig. 5 Fertilization

Pollen grain

Surface of stigma

Pollen tube

Female gamete

Ovule

Micropyle

a) Pollen grains transferred to stigma

b) Pollen germinates and produces pollen tube

Pollen tube

Male gamete

c) Pollen tube grows down style and enters ovule via micropyle, carrying the male gamete (pollen) to the female gamete

Female gamete

Male gamete

Female gamete

d) Male and female gametes fuse to form a zygote (seed)

Fig. 6 Germination

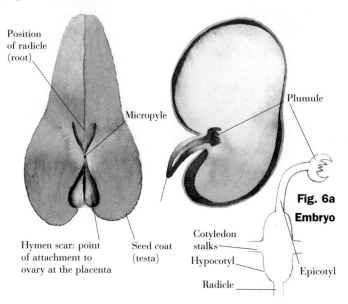

Position of radicle (root)

Micropyle

Plumule

Hymen scar: point of attachment to ovary at the placenta

Seed coat (testa)

Cotyledon stalks

Hypocotyl

Radicle

Epicotyl

Fig. 6a Embryo

titious, and the flower petals and sepals are arranged in threes or groups of three.

Seed may be either dry or moist. Dry seed must be stored in dry conditions and most dry seeds appear to benefit from a period of chilling. Do not store dry seed in plastic bags or containers; use paper envelopes and cardboard boxes kept cool.

Moist seeds (for example oak and chestnut) contain fats as well as the water content and must not be allowed to dry out, as this would either kill the seed or reinforce its dormancy. Moist seed should be put in a mix of equal parts moist sand and peat or between layers of damp sacking and stored in an open airy environment to avoid disease.

Some seeds are trapped within a pulp and can be tricky to extract. The easiest ways to do this are either through maceration – soaking the berries in water to make a liquid mash from which the seeds will float to the surface – or else by fermentation, leaving the seed in a sealed plastic bag so that the natural bacteria can break down the pulp.

When a seed does not germinate it may be that it is dormant. Dormancy can be broken in various ways: some plants require high temperatures, and exposure to fire will shatter their sleep; others need a spell of freezing or cold weather and can be stratified (mixed in moist sand and stored outside over winter or else in a refrigerator for a few weeks) to aid germination. Yet others simply need to have their hard coats broken by nicking with a sharp knife, or softened by soaking in hot water to enable the radicle, hypocotyl, and cotyledons to emerge.

Sowing seed

The sowing of seed is the most fundamental method of raising new plants, used mostly to raise hardy and half-hardy annuals and biennials for the garden, though most species of plants can be raised from seeds. Bear in mind that if the plant you are wanting to increase is a hybrid cultivar, seed saved from it will not develop to look like its parent. Instead, it will inherit some of the characteristics of one or other of its parents' parents. In fact, even seed saved from species which will come true may have enhanced leaf color or variegation, or its natural habit of growth exaggerated, and so on. This is interesting to watch for, since by careful selection you may be able to develop an especially good form of a choice plant.

The best way to sow seed is to fill a pot or tray that has been cleaned thoroughly and washed with a household disinfectant with clean, moist seed soil mix. Gently firm the soil mix into the container and then water well. Scatter the seed thinly and evenly over the surface of the soil mix and then sieve a fine layer of it over the seed. Water gently (having added fungicide to the water to help prevent the emerging seedling from damping off) and put the pot into a plastic bag or cover the tray with a sheet of glass and put in warm, but not hot, place. Light levels should be low and you can cover the trays with sheets of newspaper to ensure this. There are tabletop propagating units available that have heating cables in the base. These are very useful if you have a place to leave them plugged in.

The seed should germinate in a week to ten days. As soon as you see the seed is germinating and beginning to push through the soil, move the container into the light. If the emerging seeds do not have enough light, they will become etiolated (weak and spindly) and easily damped off.

When the first true leaves (as opposed to the cotyledons) develop, the seedlings are large enough to handle; lift them gently from the soil mix using the end of a pencil or small seedling dibble. Always hold a seedling by its leaves, never by the stem. A damaged leaf will be replaced by another, but a wounded stem condemns the plant to death.

Fig. 7 Dicotyledon Germination

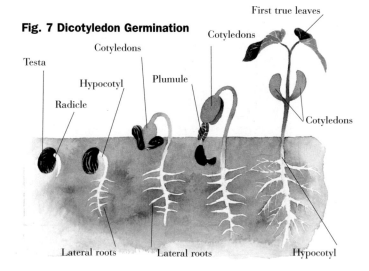

First true leaves

Cotyledons

Cotyledons

Testa

Hypocotyl

Plumule

Radicle

Cotyledons

Lateral roots

Lateral roots

Hypocotyl

Prick out the individual seedlings of large plants into individual pots; small annuals and so on can be pricked out into rows in trays. Don't overcrowd the trays; to grow into strong plants, the seedlings should be planted no less than about 1 in. (2.5 cm) apart. Overcrowding means the plants must compete for food and light. In a standard seed tray, about five plants across and six down (30 plants) is a good average.

Keep the pricked-out seedlings in the greenhouse for a few days and then, as the weather warms, harden them off by moving the trays and pots outside for a few hours each day, increasing the time they spend in the fresh air as the days become warmer. This is an essential part of the process of raising plants from seed.

Herbaceous perennials grown from seed can flower well in their second season, but there are some which will take several years to reach flowering size. Cultivars and F1 hybrids are unlikely to come true from self-saved seed but species perennials should, although as mentioned earlier there may be variation in the depth of color or leaf size. Sow the seed in spring or summer on a spare piece of ground, or else in pots set out in a cold frame. With tray-sown seed, thin the seedlings as necessary to allow for strong growth, and when the plants are large enough pot them up into 3 in. (8 cm) pots.

Take a look at the seed; if it is flat it will germinate more readily if you take the time to sow it on its side or edge. Some seeds have long "tails"; if you poke the seed into the soil mix with this tail protruding, it will spiral as it dries and in the process twist the seed firmly and deeply into the soil mix.

The Stem

Propagation from stem cuttings is the second most common method after seed; leaf cuttings are less frequently used and tend to be a means of increasing houseplants and exotic ornamentals.

Fig. 8 Monocotyledon Germination

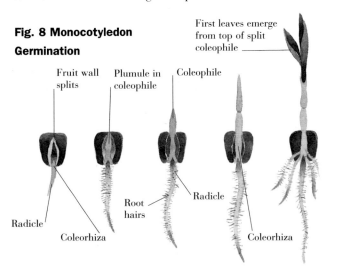

First leaves emerge from top of split coleophile

Fruit wall splits

Plumule in coleophile

Coleophile

Coleophile

Radicle

Root hairs

Radicle

Radicle

Coleorhiza

Coleorhiza

Being vegetative methods, leaf and stem cuttings are the most widely used way of producing new plants which are guaranteed to be exact replicas of the parent. In addition, where perennial plants are concerned, cuttings produce usable plants more rapidly.

Apart from providing plants with their characteristic forms and shapes, stems serve a number of basic functions. They support the leaves, flowers and buds for optimum light absorption, and to enhance the opportunities for pollination and seed dispersal; leaves are spaced along the stems to receive the best light and most oxygen possible. They are the conduit for water and nutrients from the roots to the leaves and allow for the manufacture and storage of food for all the plant tissue; although most food production (photosynthesis) takes place in the leaves, some takes place in green stems.

On a green stem (Fig. 8), the epidermis is a layer of closely fitting cells that holds the inner tissues in shape, prevents water loss, and protects the internal structures of the stem against disease and pest damage. The epidermis is punctured with microscopic lenticels through which the plant respires, exchanging oxygen for carbon dioxide. On older woody plant stems, the epidermis gives way to an outer sheath of cork that is several cell layers thick; this is the bark that makes some trees and shrubs highly decorative.

The cortex and the pith consist of large, thin-walled cells separated by air spaces to allow air to move around the tissues of the plant. The cells themselves are water receptacles, and when full help to keep the stem erect (turgid); a plant wilts as these cells empty. The cells also form protective packing around the vascular bundles of phloem and xylem; the phloem allows for the movement of photosynthesized nutrients around the plant, while water and nutrients absorbed by the roots travel to the leaves via the xylem.

The cambium is a layer of thin-walled narrow cells that divides the vascular bundles in half, separating the inner xylem layer from the outer phloem layer. Xylem and phloem are created by the cambium layer, and each year the new layer pushes the old one out, creating the characteristic tree rings seen when a branch is cross-sectioned. Cambium cells have the ability to divide and to produce adventitious roots, so it is from this layer that a cutting develops roots.

The tip of the stem is the apical bud (Fig. 9a), containing hormonal active meristem tissue. The point along a stem where the leaves are attached is called the node; meristem stem tissue is also present in the bud at the nodes, nestled between the leaf and the stem. The distance between nodes along a stem is the internode; some plants can be propagated by internodal cuttings (Fig. 10d).

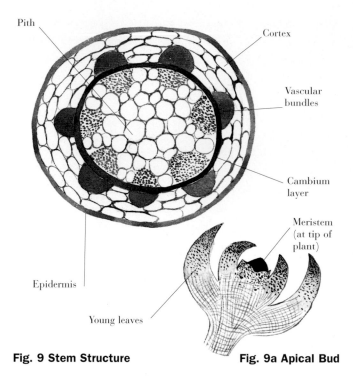

Pith

Cortex

Vascular bundles

Cambium layer

Epidermis

Meristem (at tip of plant)

Young leaves

Fig. 9 Stem Structure

Fig. 9a Apical Bud

Softwood cuttings

These are made from young green shoots. They are particularly good for propagating herbaceous perennials, and can be taken at any time in the season when there is vigorous new growth. Softwood cuttings of trees and shrubs are from the new season's growth taken during spring. Cutting material should be healthy, non-flowering shoots (a plant in flower has its hormones geared to vegetative growth and so is unlikely to produce roots). Take cuttings about 4 in. (10 cm) long, cutting them away from the parent plant just above a node. Collect the cuttings in the early morning while they are turgid; to keep the cuttings in good condition as you gather them, put them in a plastic bag into which you have sprinkled a few drops of water. It is essential to keep the cuttings moist.

Prepare pots and trays as for seed sowing, using your usual soil mix, but add some extra grit or horticultural vermiculite to give it quite an open texture. I do this even if the soil mix says it is for cuttings, adding horticultural vermiculite in a ratio of one potful of grit to two of soil mix. Newly developing roots prefer the reduced resistance of an open soil mix; damp, compacted soil mix would make the cutting rot off. Do not firm the soil mix too vigorously as both air and moisture must be present around the cutting.

To prepare the cutting, trim away the stem below the lowest node as cleanly as you can (Fig. 10a), being careful not to squash the end of the stem; I make the cut against my thumb, using a sharp scalpel and a great deal of care. A sharp knife will suffice, but do not use pruners or scissors. Next, trim away the lowest leaves and any flowers and buds, being careful not to

nick the stem. Cuttings taken during summer should have all but the uppermost two pairs of leaves removed; the reason for this is that during warm weather, leaves lose moisture. Cuttings taken late in the season and during winter or early spring should have a greater number of leaves to absorb all the light possible to continue photosynthesis. If the cutting is taken from a large-leaved plant, cut each leaf in half and dip the cut edge in disinfectant solution to prevent the disease botrytis.

When the cambium is cut it forms a callus which contains cells that differentiate between stem and root. Hormones gather at the cut, activating the root-forming cells. Dipping the cut end into hormone rooting powder or solution assists this process. Tap off any excess rooting agent; too much would kill the cutting.

Use a pencil or small dibble to put the cutting into the soil mix to about one-third of its depth; the cutting should be deep enough to be secure, with the growth point held cleanly above the soil mix. Firm the soil mix around the cuttings and water them in with a fungicide solution.

The cuttings must be kept moist, and if you are planning to produce prodigious numbers of plants you should invest in a mist-propagating unit. These have sensors which periodically engage misting sprays above the bench to ensure a constant moist atmosphere around the cuttings. The bottom of the unit will have a soil-warming cable under the layer of felt or sand on which the pots and trays stand to provide bottom heat which encourages rooting. Otherwise, cover the pots or trays with a

Fig. 10 Stem Cuttings

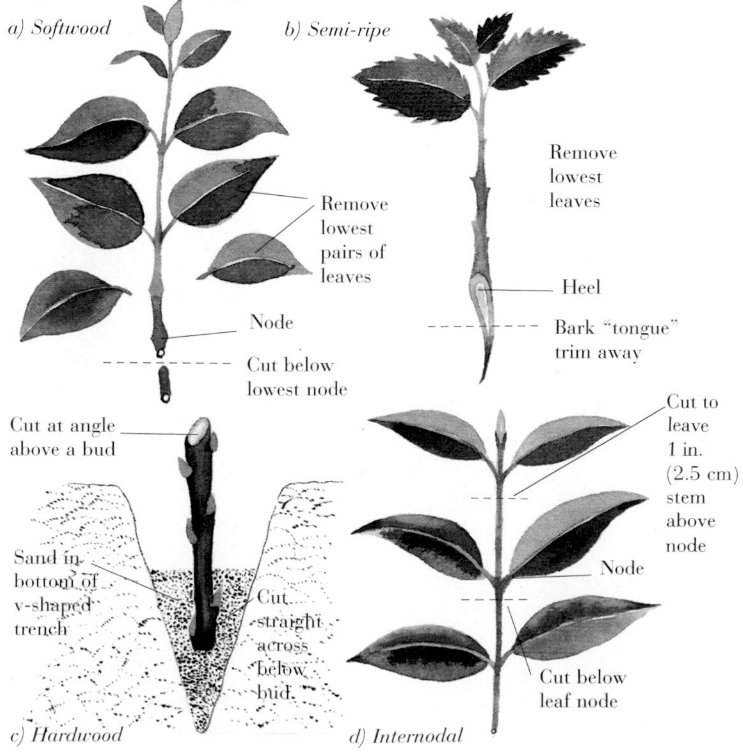

a) Softwood

b) Semi-ripe

Remove lowest pairs of leaves

Node

Cut below lowest node

Remove lowest leaves

Heel

Bark "tongue" trim away

c) Hardwood

Cut at angle above a bud

Sand in bottom of v-shaped trench

Cut straight across below bud

d) Internodal

Cut to leave 1 in. (2.5 cm) stem above node

Node

Cut below leaf node

polyethylene bag or half of a clear plastic bottle (I find the latter especially good for pots of cuttings). Both methods make a mini-greenhouse and keep a moist atmosphere around the cuttings. In summer the ambient heat may be enough but using a propagating unit with bottom heat will speed up the process.

Don't stand cuttings on the sunniest benches; put them where they will be cool and shaded. After a few weeks, tug gently on a leaf: if the cutting stays firm in the soil mix it will be rooted and can be potted up individually, placed outside in a sheltered spot to harden off and, when it has reached a suitable size, finally planted out in the garden.

Semi-ripe cuttings

These are taken at the end of summer when the new season's growth has begun to ripen and go woody near the base. Cuttings should be non-flowering and about 4-6 in. (10-15 cm) long. This type of cutting is best for woody-stemmed perennials. Pull the cutting away from the main stem, taking a small flap or "heel" of old bark at the base (which is why they are sometimes called heel cuttings). Callus forms at this heel. Trim the end of it if it is long or ragged, and remove the leaves as for soft cuttings (Fig. 10b). Dip the cut end into hormone rooting powder. Semi-ripe cuttings will root in much cooler conditions than softwood cuttings so there is no need for a propagating unit, they will do fine on the greenhouse staging.

Hardwood cuttings

This type of cutting makes use of fully mature wood of the current year's growth – hardwood cuttings should not be more than one year old. Take the cuttings from late autumn to midwinter during the plant's dormant period. If the sap is still running when the cutting is taken it may dry out, adversely affecting the cambium layer.

Hardwood cuttings are slow to root, so you must have space in your garden to leave them undisturbed for at least one year. Only a small range of plants are suitable for hardwood cuttings: roses are favorites for this treatment (although I have had more success with internodal cuttings). The cuttings should be pencil-thick and about 12–18 in. (30–45 cm) long, but take a cutting longer than you need and then trim it by cutting the top end above a node at a slant to shed rain and cutting the bottom end straight across just below a node. (The different ends also help to identify top and bottom.)

Make a V-shaped trench about 8 in. (20 cm) deep and put a 2 in. (5 cm) layer of sharp sand in the bottom to provide drainage which will help to activate the cambium. You can use hormone rooting powder, but it will need to be of higher strength than for other types of cutting. Put the cuttings into the trench

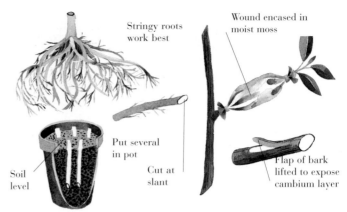

Fig. 11 Root Cuttings   **Fig. 12 Air Layering**

so that they stand upright without leaning and are at a depth of at least two-thirds their length (Fig. 10c).

Basal cuttings

Basal cuttings are taken from the new shoots that appear at the base of herbaceous perennials and shrubs in early spring. When the basal stems are an inch or so (2–3 cm) long cut them just below a leaf or joint, using a clean, sharp knife. Dip the cut ends into hormone rooting powder and put the cuttings into pots or trays of loose soil mix. Alternatively, they can be rooted in a cold frame.

Internodal cuttings

These are taken in summer from a new, healthy, non-flowering side shoot. Trim to leave 1 in. (2.5 cm) of stem above and below a leaf node selected for the healthy, fat bud it holds at the junction of the leaf and main stem (Fig. 10d). Treat as for a soft cutting, but leave at least one leaf and bud. Pot the cutting, putting the node below the surface of the soil mix. Roots will develop at the base of the node.

Division

This method of increasing your stock of a plant entails lifting it from its flowering position during its dormant period and then cutting or pulling it apart to create a number of smaller plant clumps. With age, many herbaceous perennials begin to die out in the middle of the clump but continue to develop new growth around the edges. It is from here that you take the new plants, making sure that each one has at least two or three growth points. Use an old but sharp kitchen knife to cut through woody or fibrous root masses and a pair of garden forks, back to back, to pry apart stringy-rooted clumps like hostas. Before replanting, I usually trim the roots by grasping them in a bunch near the crown of the plant and then cutting away any straggling ends that protrude.

Alternate   Opposite   Whorls

Fig. 13 Leaf Arrangements

Root cuttings

A few herbaceous plants such as oriental poppies are propagated by means of root cuttings. They are taken in late winter or when the plant has been lifted for division. Cut pieces of healthy root about 2–3 in. (5–7.5 cm) long. Cut the bottom end of the root section (the end furthest from the top growth) at a slant to identify which way is up (Fig. 11). Put thick roots vertically in pots of soil mix, lay thin roots horizontally on soil-mix-filled trays. Cover with about 1/4 in. (6 mm) of soil mix or vermiculite, and stand the containers in a cold frame or cold greenhouse. When new shoots appear the plants can be potted individually.

Runners

An easy way to propagate a number of groundcovering plants is by making cuttings from the new growths that appear at the end of long trailing stems. Saxifrages, ivy, strawberries, and mint are a few familiar runner-producing plants. Simply peg the juvenile plant at the end of the runner into a pot of soil mix, and as soon as it roots, the runner can be severed and the baby plant moved to a new home. If you wish to root many runners of one plant, just separate the babies from the parent plant, put them into a tray of soil mix, water with fungicide solution, cover, and set out in a sheltered spot. They will take root in a few weeks.

Layering

This method of propagation is useful for certain woody perennials like rhododendrons, azaleas, gardenias, and groundcover plants that root as they cover the ground. Select a branch or stem that can easily be pulled down to the ground. Make a small slit in the bark at the point where the branch touches the ground; it should be far enough from the growing tip for the latter to be held well above ground when the layering point is firmed into the soil. Dust the wound with rooting powder and peg it down on the soil using a length of bent wire or a clothes peg. Cover with soil mix, and when the new growth appears, cut the layer from the old plant and pot on until it is strong enough to plant out.

Air layering

This is similar in practice to layering except that the wounded bark is wrapped in a moist medium and the roots develop into this before being potted into soil mix. Select a healthy, straight semi-ripe side shoot and with a sharp knife make a wound by slicing along the stem towards the growing tip and then lift a narrow tongue of bark (Fig. 12). Use a toothpick to hold the flap open and dust the wound with hormone rooting compound.

Wrap the wounded portion in damp sphagnum moss and bind the moss loosely in a plastic bag. Then wrap this in plastic to prevent it from drying out, sealing both ends with plant ties. Water the main plant regularly. In several months you should see roots poking through the moss. Sever the shoot from the old plant, cutting cleanly just below the new roots, then pot it.

The Leaf

The chief function of leaves is food production, for they are the main site of photosynthesis. This is most simply expressed as the process of creating complex chemicals (sugars and oxygen) from simple ones (carbon dioxide and water) using either natural light (sunlight) or artificial light. In photosynthesis the leaf absorbs light and carbon dioxide from the atmosphere and processes them into sugars like glucose, releasing oxygen as a by-product of the chemical changes. Leaves also allow the plants to transpire, shedding excess water to cool the plant.

The three main ways in which leaves are arranged around the stem are shown in Fig. 13. Similarly, there are three main ways

Fig. 14 Leaf Types

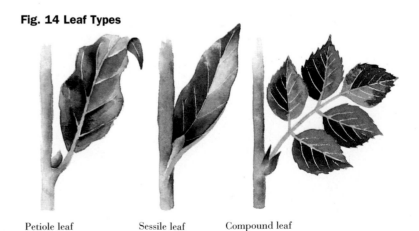

Petiole leaf   Sessile leaf   Compound leaf

Opposite. Apart from their aesthetic appeal, leaves sustain the life of a plant, provide the energy, and often the means by which it can be reproduced.

Fig. 15 Cross-section to show Leaf Structure

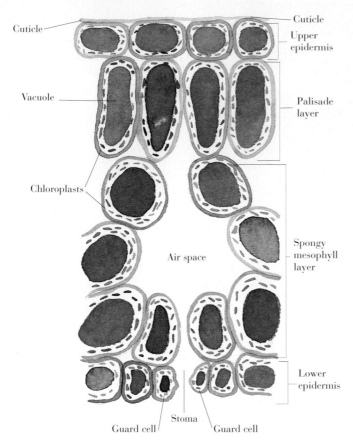

Cuticle
Cuticle
Upper epidermis
Vacuole
Palisade layer
Chloroplasts
Spongy mesophyll layer
Air space
Lower epidermis
Guard cell
Stoma
Guard cell

the pigments which give leaves their color. The spongy mesophyll are the lungs of the plant, and breathe through the stomata on the lower epidermis of the plant: in respiration, the stomata allow oxygen in and carbon dioxide out, reversing the process during photosynthesis. There are a few stomata on the upper epidermis also. The guard cells on either side of the openings also respond to moisture, opening and closing the stomata; in a moist atmosphere the stomata remain open and in dry heat they shut rapidly. That is why a constant misted atmosphere is desirable in propagation to avoid stressing the food-producing cells within the leaves as the cuttings try to establish roots.

The midribs and veins contain the vascular bundles, and thus the cambium layer needed for propagation.

Leaf blade cuttings

These are used for streptocarpus, sansevieria (mother-in-law's tongue), begonias, and Christmas and Easter cactus. Take a healthy mature leaf, place it upside-down on a clean surface and with a sterile sharp knife make small incisions across the main veins, cutting through to the other side (Fig. 16). Turn the leaf right-side up and place it on a tray of moist soil mix. To make sure that the cuts have contact with the soil mix, use a few clean pebbles to hold the leaf in place. Put the tray in a propagator; in a matter of weeks, roots will form at the cuts and new plantlets will emerge on the top of the old leaf.

Alternatively, cut the leaf into squares, making sure that a vein runs through the center of each square. Sections of begonia leaf can be laid flat on the soil mix while streptocarpus leaf cuttings can be inserted upright to half their depth. There is no need to cut the cactus leaves into pieces; simply detach a segment and put it to half its depth in soil mix.

in which the leaf is joined by its petiole to the main stem of the plant (Fig. 14) to allow the leaf to turn in the direction of the light. Leaves are designed to help the plant make the most of the growing conditions in its native habitat; for example, many tropical rainforest plants grow in low light levels, so the leaves have large, light-gathering surfaces with thick waxy cuticles to help prevent water loss in the hot atmosphere while plants in hot, dry, sunny climates often have tiny leaves, covered in oil glands to help conserve moisture.

The detailed structure of a leaf seen in cross-section through a microscope appears as layers of cells, each layer performing a separate function (Fig. 15). The uppermost layer is the cuticle, which gives the leaf resistance to water and fungal diseases. Next is the upper epidermis, made of tightly fitting square cells with a vacuole or reservoir of water in the center of each cell. When the plant is turgid the vacuoles are fully charged with water, giving the leaf support and helping the plant to retain its shape. Beneath this is the palisade layer, with more closely fitted cells, each with vacuoles at their centers, and containing chloroplasts. This is the site of photosynthetic action. The chloroplasts produce carbon dioxide, moving through the palisade layer towards the transparent epidermal layer to gather light, and also contain

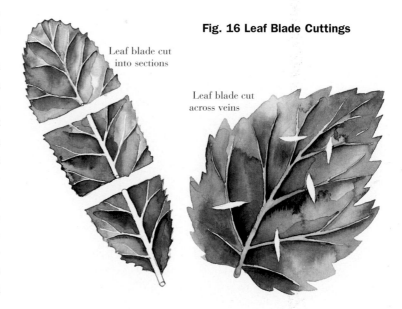

Fig. 16 Leaf Blade Cuttings

Leaf blade cut into sections

Leaf blade cut across veins

Fig. 17 Leaf Petiole Cuttings

Leaf
petiole
cutting

Fig. 18 Leaf Bud Cuttings

Apical bud

Leaf petiole cuttings

This method uses the leaf and petiole only. Select a healthy leaf and cut the petiole to about 1 in. (2.5 cm). Insert in the soil mix at a shallow angle, not upright, taking care that the leaf does not touch the soil (Fig. 17). You can put several leaves in one pot. Put the stem in so that it is held. Water with a fungicide solution and put into the propagator, shaded from direct sunlight. This method is most widely used for African violets and many other succulent plants.

Leaf bud cuttings

This is a good method of propagation when there is a shortage of healthy cutting material or the shoots from which cuttings would normally be taken have become etiolated. Leaf buds use only the section of the stem between the tip bud and uppermost leaf; this type of cutting is also sometimes called a tip cutting. Clematis, Virginia creeper, mahonias, camellias, and rubber plants are just a few of the plants that respond to this treatment. Cut the stem cleanly just below the leaf node on the uppermost leaf (Fig. 18), use hormone rooting powder, and insert the cuttings in the soil mix, several to a pot or tray. Put in a propagating unit.

Bulbs

Bulbs, corms, tubers, and rhizomes are in effect small parcels containing all the elements of growth and structure in self-con-tained underground units. The two main types of bulb are scaly bulbs such as lilies and tunicate bulbs such as daffodils and snowdrops.

Scaly bulb scales can be used for propagation (Fig. 19) remove individual scales from the bulb, insert upright into trays of moist soil mix and eventually small bulbils will form at the base of each scale. Some lilies also produce tiny bulbils along the flower stem in the leaf axils. Simply take the stem, lay it in a tray of moist soil mix, cover in a fine layer of moist grit or horticultural vermiculite, and the bulbils will develop roots. They can then be detached and grown on before planting out.

When you lift clumps of bulbs or corms you will often see mini bulbs or corms (offsets) crowding around the base (Fig. 20). Carefully remove them and set out in a nursery bed to grow on for two years, or until they are large enough to plant out in the garden.

Bulbs produced from these methods will take several years to come to flower, during which time they must be regularly fed and watered.

Fig. 19 Scaly Bulb

Bulblet
forming
on interior
of scale at
its base

Fig. 20 Tunicate Bulb

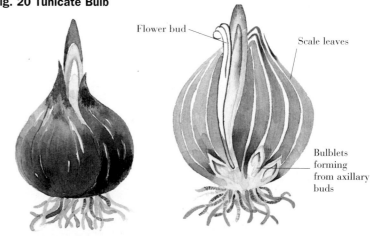

Flower bud

Scale leaves

Bulblets
forming
from axillary
buds

THE
PLANT DIRECTORY

THROUGHOUT THIS BOOK I HAVE POINTED OUT HOW important it is to suit plants to their site. When I first began gardening I tried to grow everything, regardless of whether or not I could provide the ideal conditions that the plant required. Experience, gained at the cost of countless losses of sometimes expensive plants, has taught me the error of beginner's enthusiasm (although it may have been failure that goaded me on, seeking success). Consequently, the required soil and sun conditions are given for all the plants in this index. The degrees of soil moisture range from dry to well-drained (moisture drains away rapidly), moisture-retentive (moisture remains in the soil but without making it permanently soggy), and wet (permanently soggy). The conditions of light range from full sun to semi-shade and full shade. The combinations of these conditions will determine the temperature of the soil; a dry soil in sun is more likely to be warm than a moisture-retentive soil in sun as the evaporating moisture will help to keep roots cool to some degree.

The shagbark hickory, *Carya ovata*, adds its vibrant yellow tints to the autumn show in the forests of New England, yet a mature tree is just as noteworthy for its peeling ragged bark. *Overleaf left*, flowering cherries, like *Prunus serrulata* "Shirotae" have rich autumn tints, and the berry-covered spikes of the arum lily, *Zantedeschia aethiopica (overleaf right)*, will also continue the show after flowers have faded.

All soils can be ameliorated to improve their condition, but they cannot be permanently altered. That is why I, for example, don't attempt to grow acid-loving plants on my slightly alkaline soil – I don't want to have to keep digging in peat in an effort to create acid conditions.

The entries are grouped first according to color and visual interest and then by a loose classification of annuals and perennials, shrubs and climbers, and trees. It was difficult to know where to draw the line among the plants I have included. Over the years I have developed a palette of leafy plants which remain firm favorites and have been included in each garden I have made. Some of the plants listed come highly recommended by gardening friends; there are others which I have enjoyed growing in the past, and some which I will feature in the future. I'd love to garden in the southwestern United States so that I could have

a garden full of cacti and succulents, or in Hobart, Tasmania, so that my garden could be filled with as many of the scented native shrubs as I could accumulate – and I long to grow candlebark eucalyptus! But that is what makes gardening such a pleasure, dreaming about what you could grow and will grow. No doubt some of you will discover that one or more of your favorite leaf, bark, or berry plants has been ignored (I don't have much time for ornamental conifers, for example, although I know there are some pretty ones around), but I hope I will have introduced some unfamiliar plants instead. Above all, I hope this list will encourage you to begin composing your own plant directory, to go into the garden looking not just at the flower color, but also taking in the huge variety of leaf shape, texture, and color, and the equally vibrant variations in shape and habit, bark, and berry.

YELLOW, ORANGE, RED, & PURPLE

A ground-covering mat of *Ajuga reptans* "Atropurpurea" is like a spilled bottle of old claret; the color is best in semi-shade, and makes a perfect backdrop to spring bulbs like grape hyacinths, scillas and buttery yellow primroses. When these flowers fade, the everpurple ajuga foliage remains to support its own show of blue flower spikes.

Semi-shaded or even fully shaded corners can be brightened up with the fresh acid-green spring growth of
Filipendula ulmaria "Aurea."

Annuals and perennials

Ajuga reptans is a groundcovering
perennial that has glossy green, long
oval leaves and early-summer spikes
of lilac-blue flowers. "Atropurpurea"
is dark vinous purple; "Catlin's Giant"
has large, brownish-purple leaves;
"Burgundy Glow" has cream-edged
rose and purple coloring; "Multicolor"
has bronze-green leaves splashed with
pink and white and "Variegata" has
pale green leaves blotched with cream.
Propagate from rooted runners. It likes
moisture-retentive soil in semi-shade.

Cordyline australis is one of the garden
designer's favorite architectural plants,
popularly used as a specimen plant in
urns and formal containers or else as a
sort of living sculpture in borders and
vistas. In cold zones give it winter
protection or put it under glass. An
evergreen perennial, it comes in a range
of warm tints; the names "Sundance,"
"Torbay Dazzler," and "Torbay Red"
give some idea of colors. It requires well-
drained soil in sun.

Filipendula ulmaria "Aurea" is the
brightest tinted form of meadowsweet;

the palmate leaves are acid green and
the plant makes a bright mound in a
shady corner of the springtime garden.
The color deepens as the flower stalks
appear in midsummer. Propagate by
division. A hardy perennial, it requires
moisture-retentive soil in semi-shade.

Geranium sessiliflorum "Nigricans" is
a good ground-hugging geranium with
thumbnail-sized brown leaves sprinkled
over in midsummer with small white
flowers. It self-sows admirably so will
soon colonize, especially if grown in
gravel. It mingles beautifully with brown

Humulus lupulus "Aureus" *(left)* is the golden-leaved hop, a perennial climber that will quickly cover trellis or wire supports. It can be grown through trees and evergreens, but is quite aggressive so should be thinned when the shoots first begin to climb. The black-leaved lily turf, *Ophiopogon planiscapus* "Nigrescens" *(right)*, is among the plants which will provide the darkest foliage tints year-round; its dwarf cousin *O. japonicus* "Minor" makes a good substitute for grass turf in hot arid conditions, and can be used to edge paving.

grasses like *Carex comans* bronze form or blue *Festuca glauca*. Propagate from cuttings taken in summer. It is an extremely easy perennial, preferring well-drained soil in sun and even tolerating drought conditions.

***Houttuynia cordata* "Chameleon"** is a charming water's edge groundcover with heart-shaped leaves blotched with red and cream; the variegation is improved if the plant gets a few hours of sun each day. It is quite vigorous and will quickly carpet a boggy bank, carrying little white starry flowers in summer.

Propagate by division in spring. This hardy perennial likes moisture-retentive soil in sun or semi-shade.

***Humulus lupulus* "Aureus"** is the golden hop, with the same vigorous climbing habit of the species but with bright canary-yellow juvenile foliage, becoming gradually greener with age. Propagate from basal cuttings or by division. This perennial climber likes well-drained soil in semi-shade.

***Lysimachia nummularia* "Aurea"** (moneywort, creeping jenny) A vigorous,

evergreen groundcover plant with round yellow leaves. Propagate by division in spring; plant in a moisture-retentive soil in semi-shade.

***Milium effusum* "Aureum"** (Bowles's golden grass) This has the most satisfyingly canary-yellow leaves, long, broad, and rather limp, and in midsummer similarly colored erect stems topped by elegant open panicles of dainty flowers. It spreads slowly by underground rhizomes and also seeds itself around, coming true from seed; a colony makes pools of sunlight in a woodland planting.

Lysimachia nummularia "Aurea" *(left)* rapidly makes a tightly woven blanket of small leaves and can be clipped back to keep it in check. *Phormium tenax (right)* offers a wide color range in its strap-like leaves and being tall in stature makes a good feature plant.

It can also be propagated by division. It likes moisture-retentive soil in shade.

***Ophiopogon planiscapus* "Nigrescens"** This grass-like perennial is a real curiosity for the squid's-ink blackness of its curving strap-like leaves. It makes a good companion for blue-flowered plants and brown and rust-colored foliage plants. Propagate from the creeping rhizomes and plant in a well-drained soil in sun or semi-shade.

***Origanum vulgare* "Aureum"** is the golden-leaved form of the herb marjoram, a creeping groundcover that makes a vivid yellow carpet of tiny round leaves topped by a thin dusting of pale mauve flowers in summer. Propagate by division. This hardy perennial likes a well-drained soil in sun.

Perilla frutescens is an oriental herb known in the West as the "beefsteak plant" (use it in salads or stir-fries as you would spinach). The dark purple-black leaves and stems make it a good "dot" plant in bedding schemes, and the rough seersucker surface of the glossy leaves seems to reflect light to an extent unusual in a dark foliage plant. This is a half-hardy annual; raise from seed sown under glass in early spring for planting out after frosts, or else sow in succession in the vegetable garden when the soil has warmed. It likes well-drained soil in sun.

Phormium The Purpureum group of *P. tenax* offer a good bronze-purple color and strong vertical accent from the stiff sword-like leaves. There are a number of cultivars with other tints of rose, cream, verdigris, and mauve, including *P. cookianum* ssp. *hookeri* "Cream Delight" and "Tricolor," *P. tenax* "Variegatum"

Ricinus communis "Gibsonii" is a real "mega-star" among foliage plants for the size of its palmate leaves and luscious coloring; tropical gardeners can grow it easily, but temperate gardeners must exercise their passion by overwintering it under glass, only bringing it outdoors for the summer to grace a tropical-themed border with other exotics like canna lilies. It is, however, poisonous, so use with care.

and *P.* "Sundowner," the names giving an indication of the coloring. Propagate by division in autumn or early spring. These hardy perennials require well-drained soil in sun or semi-shade.

Rheum palmatum **"Atrosanguineum"** is the best form of the ornamental rhubarb, with broad deeply lobed and serrated leaves that are burgundy red when young, turning a pleasing emerald green as they age. Rosy-pink flower spikes tower above the foliage clump in early summer. It is also useful at the water's edge, where its bold silhouette is

caught in the reflecting water. Propagate by division in spring. This hardy perennial will grow in any soil in sun.

Ricinus communis (castor-oil plant) has broad palmate leaves with serrated edges colored, like the stems, a striking shade of glossy cordovan red. "Gibsonii" is a compact variety with bronze foliage. This is a fast-growing plant that is perennial in only the warmest zones, but can be grown as an annual elsewhere. A "must-have" for a tropical border planting, but note that it is poisonous. It requires moisture-retentive soil in sun.

Salvia officinalis "Kew Gold" and "Icterina" are the yellow forms of common sage; the first has the brightest, pure yellow young growth, while the second is splashed with yellow variegation. Propagate from cuttings in late summer. These are hardy shrubs that like a well-drained soil in sun.

Rodgersia podophylla makes a stunning statement of form and texture at the water's edge, with broad palmate leaves, deeply toothed and rich bronze in color, fading to shining green with age. All this splendor is topped by panicles of tiny

Clockwise from top left, the bold leaves of *Rodgersia podophylla* have a strongly defined shape and so make a good contrast plant to finer textured foliage like the lacy claret-tinted leaves of *Acer palmatum* "Dissectum Atropurpureum," the heptalobum acer "Ozakazuki," and *Berberis thunbergii* "Red Pillar," all of which enjoy moisture-retentive soils.

white flowers in summer. *R. sambucifolia* has compound palmate leaves that are glowing emerald green, but shaded with bronze as they age. Propagate by division of rhizomatous clumps in autumn. These hardy perennials like moisture-retentive soil in sun.

Shrubs and climbers

Acer palmatum (Japanese maple) There are numerous named cultivars and varieties within this group of deciduous shrubs, with *A. p.* "Dissectum Atropurpureum" probably the most popular for its low-spreading, densely mounded habit and deeply cut palmate foliage with a fine ferny look. Its leaves are dark mahogany purple while *A. p.* "Dissectum Variegatum" has leaves mottled shrimp pink, cream, and green. They produce the best color on neutral or slightly acid soil, and require a moist soil in sun but will tolerate some shade.

Acer palmatum **var.** *heptalobum* This variety within the Japanese maples contains many colorful medium-sized shrubs which are larger in stature in every way to the dissectums, although the foliage retains the deeply lobed and delicate appearance. "Heptalobum Elegans" leaves fade from ruby red to pink with age while "Linearilobum Atropurpureum" has coppery-red leaves. Plant in moist soil in sun or semi-shade.

Berberis thunbergii **"Red Pillar"** is an attractive form with red-purple leaves turning scarlet in autumn. It requires well-drained soil in sun or shade. Propagate from semi-ripe cuttings.

Cotinus **spp.** *C. coggygria* "Royal Purple" and *C.* "Flame" and *C.* "Grace"

The smoke bush *Cotinus coggygria (left)*, has many cultivars each with its own distinctive tint of purple-red. Hard pruning after flowering will encourage larger leaves, but left alone, it will make a large open shrub that works well in a mixed border with old shrub roses.

are all good forms of the smoke bush, so called for the billowing, hazy effect of the flowerheads. "Royal Purple" has the darkest coloring. The best foliage is produced on plants that are coppiced in late autumn or winter. *C. obovatus*, the American smoke tree, is taller growing and colors in autumn from plum-purple to hot gold and russet red. Propagate by semi-ripe cuttings in late summer and plant these medium-sized shrubs in moisture-retentive soil in sun.

Gleditsia triacanthos (honey locust) Grow the cultivar "Sunburst" for its

bright yellow pinnate leaves that change gradually to soft green as they age. It is a small deciduous tree but is best grown as a large shrub by pruning hard each winter after leaf fall to encourage a vivid display. The wood is quite brittle, and keeping it low will help to avoid wind damage. It likes a well-drained soil in full sun, will grow on limestone and can withstand periods of drought.

Nandina domestica Semi-evergreen small shrub with leaves tinged red and purple in spring and autumn. Propagate from semi-ripe cuttings in late summer.

Requires a sheltered position and well-drained soil.

Trees

Catalpa bignonioides "Aurea" (Indian bean tree) Big, broad, heart-shaped leaves and bold trusses of outsize snapdragon-like flowers followed by 12 in. (30 cm) long pendent "beans" make this a dramatic large specimen tree. The brightness of the yellow deciduous leaves (up to 8 in. [20cm] long and wide) just serves to emphasize its presence. It will grow in any soil in sun.

The golden-leaved Indian bean tree, *Catalpa bignonioides* "Aurea" *(center)*, makes a stunning specimen tree in a large garden. Everything about the tree is "big" – from the flower candelabras to the pendent "bean" seedpods, and the large leaves which give it a coarse, eye-catching texture. *Nandina domestica (right)*, creates thickets in the forest understory and so makes a good medium-height filler plant beneath trees and between taller growing shrubs.

Cercis canadensis (Judas tree) is a lovely addition to the springtime garden, underplanted with daffodils or bluebells; the pink flowers nestle amid the pink-tinged heart-shaped leaves, which take on a more greenish cast as they age. The foliage of *C. c.* "Forest Pansy" colors purple in the autumn, and in both forms the fallen leaves have an unmistakable warm scent of candy floss. It is a small deciduous tree that likes moist soil (preferably acid) in sun.

Fagus sylvatica "Rohanii" (purple fernleaf beech) has deeply laciniate leaves, while *F. s.* "Purpurea Pendula" offers purple foliage and an attractive weeping habit of growth. Unless you appreciate looming dark masses, I recommend keeping purple-leaved subjects to a supporting role in the garden and working them in among brighter-colored trees. These are large deciduous trees that will grow in any soil in sun.

Prunus cerasifera "Pissardii" (syn. *P. c.* "Atropurpurea") Even though this is a paler purple than the inky "Nigra" it still has a rather glum effect. However, teamed with some incendiary reds and oranges, its somber effect can be relieved. It is a medium-sized deciduous tree that likes well-drained soil in sun and does well on alkaline soils.

Robinia pseudoacacia "Frisia" is the rich yellow-leaved form of the black locust; the deciduous leaves are pinnate, giving the tree a fluffy prettiness. The color is good from spring through late autumn, making this a valuable brightener for the garden. Although it is small it requires careful positioning as it is thorny. It will grow in any soil in sun and tolerates dry conditions.

GREEN

Since Classical times, the glossy acanthus leaf has served as architectural ornament; think of it in this context
when placing *Acanthus mollis* in the garden.

The feather-like fronds of *Adiantum pedatum (left)* are strikingly marked by the shiny black stalks that carry each delicate leaflet or pinnule; it grows easily in any moist, humus-rich soil in shade. *Astilboides tabularis (right)* is another moist-shade lover, but its leaves are more substantial, making a good groundcover among shade-loving spring flowers.

Annuals and perennials

***Acanthus* spp.** (bear's breeches)
A hardy perennial, semi-evergreen in sheltered areas, with large leathery leaves and architectural flower spikes. *A. mollis*'s large mid-green leaves have a heart-shaped base; *A. spinosa*'s leaves are finely cut and spiny. Propagate by root cuttings in late autumn/winter or by seed. Position in well-drained soil in sun or semi-shade.

Adiantum venustum is a deciduous perennial fern that naturalizes in damp shady corners in mild regions. It has lacy foliage; *A. pedatum* is a hardy, woodland fern, growing in the Aleutian Islands and the cool moist gardens of North America and Europe. Propagate from divisions taken in spring. It prefers acid soil in semi-shade.

***Aruncus dioicus* "Kneiffii"** makes a clump of the finest, laciest foliage of any perennial; each leaf is deeply cut, with the edges serrated and colored a mild green. It has a stiff, branching habit and in midsummer is topped by a frothy plume of starry white flowers. Propagate by division in autumn. Position in well-drained soil in sun or semi-shade.

Asplenium scolopendrium (syn. *Phyllitis scolopendrium*) This is the common woodland hart's tongue fern, of which there are numerous forms; the Crispum group offers dainty plants with attractively crinkled edges to the tongue-shaped leaves. Propagate by division of the crown in spring and plant in moist, alkaline soil in semi-shade.

Astilboides tabularis is a hardy perennial with bright green umbrella-

Gardeners in temperate climates are hard pushed for mammoth-leaved plants, but *Gunnera manicata* fits the bill perfectly; well-grown in a water's edge site, or else in humus-rich, moisture-retentive soil it will make a clump easily 8 ft. (2.5 m) tall. The species *G. chilensis*, found as far south as Patagonia, is a degree or two hardier but still appreciates heavy winter mulching.

shaped leaves. Propagate by division of rhizomes in spring. Requires moist soil in semi-shade.

Gunnera manicata is probably one of the greatest glories of water's edge planting; the leaves on a mature plant can be as much as 5 ft. (1.5 m) across – and this plant is a herbaceous perennial! It is not entirely frost hardy, so in cold zones it should be heavily mulched during winter by folding the fading leaves over the crown and then covering in a thick layer of straw or other mulch material. This plant requires moist soil

in sun or semi-shade. Propagate by division of new crowns in spring.

Lysichiton camtschatcensis and ***L. americanus*** are bog or water plants which have white or yellow spathes respectively wrapped around the poker of inconspicuous flowers; these appear in early spring and are followed by long, broadly tapering leaves glossy in texture and emerald green in color. Don't be put off by the common name of skunk cabbage – they are real stunners for the stream or water garden. Propagate by division in spring. These are hardy

perennials that need wet soil in sun or semi-shade.

Matteuccia struthiopteris, commonly known as ostrich fern, has its erect, bright green fronds arranged like a shuttlecock, which is its other alias. Propagate by division of the rhizomatous root in spring. This deciduous fern requires moist soil in semi-shade.

Musa basjoo (banana) and ***M. acuminata*** (blood banana) are admirable foliage plants where a pronounced exotic effect is desired.

Matteuccia struthiopteris revels in damp shady or semi-shaded places and is especially well-suited to bog garden plantings where the constant level of moisture and humid conditions are just to its liking. In such a spot it can be invasive, but it is worth tolerating this for the soft visual effect of the feathery fronds. Try to plant it so that the low evening light will illuminate the foliage for a brief, brilliant moment.

They are tropical plants, so you must have the space and warmth to accommodate them if you live anywhere north of the Equator – and the strength to move them, as they can grow to quite a size. The blood banana gets its name for the wine-red coloring of the central rib and stem of the long, flat, oval leaves; it looks terrific planted with canna lilies and the coppery-red *Ricinus communis (see page 102)*. These perennials require a sunny position, frequent feeding during the growing period and deeply dug moisture-retentive soil, enriched with plenty of organic matter, to do well.

Polystichum setiferum (soft shield fern) has long feathery evergreen fronds that curve gently at the tips. "Divisilobum Densum" has a curious fuzzy look about it because of the finely divided, densely crowded fronds; the color is a pleasing soft green and the midrib caramel brown. Propagate by division of the rhizomes. It requires moisture-retentive soil in semi-shade.

***Stipa* spp.** This genus of mainly perennial clump-forming grasses has about 300 species, of which there is space here only to mention those that are in my

opinion the best. *S. arundinacea*, a native of Australia and New Zealand, makes a 3–4 ft. (0.9–1.2 m) tall clump of slender arching leaves that move with sinuous grace in the slightest breeze and take on a golden-russet glow in late autumn. In late summer the flowers form in loose open panicles that create a fine film above the steadily reddening foliage. *S. gigantea* is widely available and deserves its popularity for the erect 5 ft. (1.5 m) tall flowering stems that sway above the grassy hummocks of mid-green narrow leaves. These inflorescences appear in early summer

Used in a pool-side planting, the glimmering leaves of *Zantedeschia aethiopica* "Crowborough" echo the glistening surface of the water. Although it likes being planted in water, it will grow in any moisture-retentive soil. This form is hardy enough to grow outdoors year-round even in cool gardens, but nevertheless will benefit from having its rhizomatous roots deeply mulched.

and retain their beauty over a long season; the seed spikes become increasingly golden brown, and if positioned to catch the sun, will glisten in the breeze. *S. tenuissima* has what is probably the finest foliage and flowers among the grasses; each leaf and flower stem is as slender as silken thread and as the seedheads ripen the plant takes on a soft wheaten glow. It only reaches about 18 in. (45 cm) and looks splendid grown with the daisy-flowered *Anthemis* "E. C. Buxton" as seen in Beth Chatto's superb gravel garden in Essex, England. Propagate by division in the spring or by seed sown when ripe at the end of summer. They require well-drained soil in sun.

Veratrum nigrum is a hardy perennial better known for the curious pleating of its young foliage than for the tall, erect flower spikes bearing unusual chocolate-colored blooms. As the broad, tapering leaves begin to unfurl in early summer they have the crumpled delicacy of the fabled silken Fortuny textiles, with each frond deeply pleated. They look their best then, as the foliage begins to lose the pronounced texturing as it ages. A native of the woodland edge, this plant can be propagated by division of the crowns in early spring or from self-sown seedlings, though it takes quite a few years for seedlings to develop to a moveable size. It likes moisture-retentive soil in semi-shade.

Zantedeschia aethiopica **"Crowborough"** (arum lily) A hardier form of this half-hardy perennial with mid- to deep green, glossy arrow-shaped leaves. Propagate by offsets in winter. Plant in moisture-retentive soil in sun or semi-shade.

The evergreen ivy is a perennial favorite and *Hedera helix* "Green Ripple" *(center)*, with its deeply lobed and clearly veined leaves, is one of the more striking green-leaved sorts; it can be grown as a groundcover in woodland gardens or as a wall-trained plant. *Ilex cornuta* "Burfordii" *(right)* has only a single spine at the tip of each shiny oval leaf, making it rather more garden-friendly than some – a useful feature in a garden where children play.

Shrubs and climbers

Eriobotrya japonica (loquat) This large deciduous shrub bears curious pear-shaped yellow fruit, though these only appear if there is enough summer heat to encourage the heavily scented flowers to emerge. However, the long, tapering, leathery leaves make this an attractive shrub which looks best against a wall. Propagate from semi-ripe cuttings in late summer and grow in any soil in sun.

Hedera helix **vars** "Green Ripple" is named for the rippling mid- to light green of its strongly veined leaves and valued for its branching habit. "Conglomerata" is one of the most curious of the small-leaved evergreen ivies, known for its rigidly erect habit of growth and the way the leaves are held stiffly in evenly spaced parallel ranks along the stems. Increase from cuttings in late summer and plant in moisture-retentive soil in semi-shade.

Hydrangea sargentiana The leaves, stems and flowerheads of this not entirely hardy hydrangea are covered in downy hairs, giving the whole shrub a foggy, soft-focus look. Because of its tenderness, it is best given wall protection. It makes a tall shrub and should be planted in moisture-retentive soil in semi-shade.

Ilex **spp.** Of the evergreen shrubs, the hollies, with their light-reflecting glossy leaves, are real attention-getters. Depending on the cultivar, the berries range in color from deep red to bright yellow; you must plant a male and female to have berries. There are dozens of species and named cultivars to choose from: *I. cornuta* "Burfordii" is a dense,

Magnolia grandiflora (above), with its fleshy flowers and sturdy leathery leaves, has a demanding presence and is often used as a specimen tree in formal, Italianate gardens. But no tree surpasses *Cupressus sempervirens (opposite)* for instantly summoning up visions of Mediterranean gardens. It is the strongest vertical element in the fabled landscapes of Classical and Renaissance gardens, and is widely used today, as here in the south of France at La Casella to create formal avenues and vistas.

compact female form with entire or spiny leaves, *I. aquifolium* "Green Pillar" is an erect, narrow female form with dark green spiny leaves, "Myrtifolia" is a male shrub with small dark green leaves and variable spining while "Pyramidalis" has green stems and bright green slightly spiny leaves. Increase by softwood cuttings in late summer. Any soil in sun or shade will suffice.

Magnolia grandiflora Fabled for its vast creamy white waxy flowers and heady perfume, this large tree has evergreen foliage quite as striking as the

blooms. Large, glossy dark green ovals (often with reddish-brown felt beneath) provide a perfect setting for the white flowers; in warm zones it grows happily as a tree (seeing rows of young trees covered in shining leaves and perfect flowers lined out in Italian nurseries at Pistoia is a sight for sore eyes) but in colder regions it is best trained as a large shrub against a warm wall. "Undulata" has distinctly veined leaves with wavy margins that are glossy green above and green beneath even when immature. These plants require well-drained soil in sun and are tolerant of

a limestone base, provided there is a good depth of loam.

Trees

Alnus glutinosa "Imperialis" is the most distinguished member of the alders. A medium-sized deciduous tree with very finely cut leaves, it should perhaps be helped with a little pruning to take a more stately posture than it typically would; many trees respond well to this sort of treatment. Yellow catkins add to its charms in early spring. It will thrive in any soil in sun or semi-shade.

The use of tender exotics in cool temperate gardens expands the range of foliage you can use but also increases the challenge; the Australian native man fern, *Dicksonia antarctica (left)*, is one such plant, its fibrous trunk and long fronds evoking the primeval jungle. With fig trees like *Ficus carica (above)*, however, the warm spicy scent of the foliage and large leather leaves designed to withstand heat and drought bring to mind sunny Mediterranean gardens.

Azara microphylla Tiny round dark green leaves are neatly arrayed along the fanned-out branches of this large evergreen shrub or small tree, most often grown as a wall-trained specimen. In the earliest days of spring tiny lily-vanilla-scented flowers nestle in the leaf axils, cheering up a cold gray border. It will grow in any soil in sun or semi-shade.

Cupressus sempervirens (Italian cypress) This is one of the most evocative plants I know, calling to mind the sensual pleasures of Tuscan gardens and warm Italian nights scented with lime flowers and loud with crickets. In cold gardens these statuesque evergreens are not dependably hardy, but they will be happy enough in containers. They grow to a great age and height in the right conditions, becoming increasingly bare at the base as they mature. Plant in well-drained soil in sun.

Dicksonia antarctica is the Australian man fern, so called because it is the size of a man in its native habitat, though it can grow to as much as 30 ft. (10 m). It has a mysterious primeval aura, and its presence in a garden adds a definite touch of class. It is not fully hardy, so will need protection in all but the mildest gardens. The deeply divided evergreen fronds spring from the top of the stubby trunk, which is covered in a sort of coconut-fiber hairiness. As the fronds fade they droop down, wrapping themselves around the trunk. Although it is hard to resist tidying them up, these should be left to provide a sort of mulch protection around the trunk, helping it to conserve moisture and endure the cold. In dry spells it is necessary to mist the fern on a regular basis. It requires moisture-retentive soil in semi-shade.

The groundcovering evergreen branches of *Juniperus communis* "Repanda" *(left)* serve as a living mulch in woodland gardens; it is one of the most popular junipers and is widely grown. Portugese laurel, *Prunus lusitanica (right)*, enjoys similar popularity and, with its red leaf stems and small curved leaves, is preferable to the coarser cherry laurel, *P. laurocerasus*.

Fagus sylvatica **"Aspleniifolia"** (fern-leaf beech) is even more lovely than the common beech, with which it shares a languid drooping habit and soft autumn coloring. The deeply cut leaves give this large deciduous tree special presence, so use it as a feature plant. It will grow in any soil in sun.

Ficus carica The fig is a curiously unruly plant; it is most often seen growing against a warm wall with its feet encased in concrete-sided pits to try to control its growth by restricting root development (a method which in my garden has failed completely). However, I have seen it growing elegantly in a small grove of a dozen trees, neatly pruned to uniform mop-headed shapes. The large, leathery, deeply lobed deciduous leaves have an equally curious scent you cither love or hate. The drooping branches will root where they touch the ground, or new plants can be raised from semi-ripe cuttings in late summer. It likes well-drained soil in sun.

Juniperus spp. and cultivars

Evergreens give backbone to a garden, and none more so than the junipers, which range from tall-growing trees to shrubs or dwarf specimens for rockery gardens. Generally speaking they are a slow-growing group of trees with the exception of the widely available *J. scopulorum* "Skyrocket," which starts off with a trim conical shape, but as it ages begins to lean and open up. For pencil shapes, *J. communis* offers several good cultivars: "Hibernica" is very popular, as is the form *suecica*, and the really slow grower, "Compressa"; *J. chinensis* "Columnaris Glauca" makes a small vertical tree. For low-spreading shapes, *J. communis* "Hornibrookii" is

Taxus baccata, the evergreen English yew, has been used in gardens since the earliest times. Because it responds well to pruning it was, and remains, popular for topiary work; the tightly clipped fastigiate specimens shown here are part of a row of one dozen similarly trained yews forming a feature known as the "The Apostle Yews" in the gardens of Dartington Hall, in south-west England.

ground-hugging and slow to creep. *J. × media* "Pfitzeriana" spreads upwards and out to form a broad-headed shrub. Feathery, drooping foliage effects come from the graceful *J. recurva* var. *coxii* (which is not all that hardy) and *J. sabina* "Tamariscifolia." Junipers are good on alkaline soils but will grow in any well-drained soil in sun or semi-shade.

Prunus lusitanica (Portuguese laurel) is a most amenable evergreen tree or large shrub; it can be clipped as a tight hedge, trained to make a mop-headed standard as a showier alternative to the more

widely seen *Laurus nobilis* (sweet bay), or simply left to its own devices to make a loose rounded shrub or small tree. The leaves are dark and glossy and the petiole stems tinted red, giving it a pleasing aspect. Plant it in well-drained soil in sun or semi-shade.

Quercus castaneifolia **"Greenspire"** is an oak with a useful columnar habit and glossy green, serrated leaves; it is not truly evergreen, but does keep its leaves well into the winter. A real evergreen is *Q. ilex*, the holm or evergreen oak, which is so reminiscent of the Italian

landscape. It can be left to grow to its large, naturally shaggy domed head, or else pruned and trained to form neat topiary and hedges. The leaves are glossy dark green with silvered undersides, so that the effect is rather dusty-looking. Few trees give a better dark mass in the garden. Plant in a well-drained soil in sun.

Taxus **spp.** One of the oldest evergreens in cultivation, the yew has a mythical role in the history of gardens, as well as a highly valued position as one of the finest shrubs from which to create a

Trachycarpus fortunei, the Chusan palm, is another one of those exotic plants so tempting to cool-climate gardeners; fortunately it will withstand some frost if it is well-grown. The ribbed fans are particularly structural and so the plant makes a fine single lawn specimen, one that could be spotlit to carry the garden interest through the hours of evening darkness.

perimeter or background hedge. The dense inky green of the common yew, *T. baccata*, shows up the brighter colors of ornamental flowers and foliage plants like no other shrub and bears red fruit. *T. b.* "Fastigiata" (Irish yew) is a good dark green and is often chosen to make an evergreen vertical but with advanced age becomes rather pear-shaped, although pruning and tying in the branches to prevent them spreading can help to retain the slender shape. *T. b.* "Dovastoniana" with black-green leaves will make a small tree with long, horizontally spreading branches and a weeping habit, while *T. b.* "Lutea" is an attractive form offering eye-catching yellow berries against somber dark foliage. Hedging plants are often raised from seed but then the plants will all be different; it is much better to raise plants from cuttings taken in summer. Yews will grow in any soil in sun or semi-shade. The yew is a poisonous plant and so should never be planted to hedge an area adjacent to grazing pasture; children may find the crimson fruits tempting to eat, so exercise extreme caution before introducing this plant into your garden.

Trachycarpus fortunei is the exotic-looking Chusan palm, among the hardiest of the fan palms, which are generally a hardy bunch anyway. The leaves are glossy green fans which persist for many years and as they drop away leave the trunk with a hairy brown covering typical of so many palms. Small yellow flowers are borne in large panicles in early summer followed by blue-black fruits. It will withstand some frost but not continued freezing conditions, so it is best to offer some protection in winter. It is an evergreen medium-sized tree that likes well-drained soil in sun.

GRAY-GREEN

Each spectral gray leaf of *Agave parryi* is tipped with a small black thorn and edged with dark spines enhancing the pronounced sculptured lines of the succulent rosette. A single characterful plant can transform a planting scheme.

In early spring, the fresh young growth of *Artemisia ludoviciana* "Silver Queen" *(left)* is one of the brightest spots in the garden, making carpets of shimmering white among bulbs and other emerging silver leaves such as the statuesque cardoon, *Cynara cardunculus (right)*.

Annuals and perennials

***Agave* spp.** *A. americana* is a highly ornamental evergreen succulent that can grow to an enormous size given time and plenty of sunny warmth. This has been a popular sculptural plant in gardens since it was first introduced from the New World by a conquistador with a good eye for gardenworthy plants. In European gardens it is most often seen in a container, though in tropical gardens it can be part of a permanent planting scheme. There are three variegated forms: "Marginata," "Mediopicta," and "Variegata." *A. parryi* is described on page 118. Propagate from offsets and plant in a well-drained soil in sun.

***Artemisia ludoviciana* "Silver Queen"** (white sage) A hardy perennial with gray lance-shaped leaves which colonizes with creeping roots. Propagate by division in autumn or spring. Good groundcover for well-drained soil and full sun.

Athyrium niponicum* var. *pictum is a particularly attractive variety of the painted fern, so called for the silvery frosting that overlays each deeply divided purple-tinged frond. The deciduous foliage is soft and the plant creeps along gently, seeking sheltered spots for its not quite hardy rootstock. Propagate by division in spring and plant in moist soil in shade.

Cynara cardunculus is the cardoon, a near relative of the artichoke. Among gray-leaved plants it is one of the most architectural, standing nearly 6½ft. (2 m) tall in the sunny position and rich soil it prefers. Each leaf can be at least 3 ft. (90 cm) long and it looks best in early summer; a good companion for old-

Gray-leaved plants provide some of the finest textures in the garden; *Sedum spectabile* "Autumn Joy" *(left)* has tight rosettes of slightly frilled fleshy leaves while the felted texture of *Stachys byzantina (right)* adds soft radiance to underplantings amid spring-flowering shrubs and early perennials.

fashioned roses or as a punctuation point in the border. In late summer it will produce tall flowering stalks bearing the artichoke-shaped flowers tipped with rich mauve bristles. Do not position where the sharp spines which sometimes appear on the leaf serrations will be a danger. Propagate from offsets in spring. A herbaceous perennial, it requires well-drained soil in sun; protect at the base with a mulch in cold zones.

Helleborus × sternii The leathery pedate leaves of hellebores are evergreen and make pleasing rounded mounds,

providing good backgrounds to later-flowering plants. This form has large, open leaf fronds and each individual leaf is prettily netted over with silver veins against a pale green ground, giving the plant an attractive silvery sheen. It requires well-drained soil in sun.

Lychnis coronaria is a traditional cottage-garden hardy perennial best known for the fuchsia-pink flowers that appear in midsummer. However, throughout spring and early summer it is a spreading clump of narrow felted silvery-gray leaves, gradually taking on

height to about 18 in. (45 cm), turning the plant into a useful vertical accent. Propagate from seed. It prefers sun to shade and will grow in any soil.

Sedum spp. *S. spectabile* is the most common of the succulent sedum tribe, making a clump of oval leaves and becoming a rounded mass of flowering stalks, 18 in. (45 cm) tall by midsummer. "Autumn Joy" carries the typical gray-green leaves; *S. caucasicum* makes a sprawling clump of stems bearing gray-green leaves shaped like clam shells; *S. ruprechtii* has a similar sharply defined

The lanceolate leaves of *Elaeagnus angustifolia (left)* are cut from fine silver plate while the stems are dipped in bronze, and the scented golden flowers become amber beads, or so it would seem. The oleaster is a common shrub in shelter belt plantings, particularly in seaside gardens. The tender shrub *Melianthus major (right)* makes a strong feature plant, useful in container planting schemes.

character and the leaves take on a purple tinge as the summer ends. Propagate these herbaceous perennials by division in autumn and plant in dry soil in sun.

Stachys byzantina (lamb's ears) A hardy groundcovering perennial with woolly, felted gray leaves. "Silver Carpet" is a non-flowering variety. Propagate by division from autumn to spring. Plant in a well-drained soil in sun or semi-shade.

Verbascum olympicum (giant mullein) is a short-lived perennial that is most

often grown as a biennial. It sows itself freely around the garden, so you will never be without its great rosettes of heavily felted silvery gray leaves. *V. bombyciferum* is perhaps a whiter shade of pale gray. Propagate from seed sown in the summer to flower the following year. They like a well-drained soil in sun.

Shrubs and climbers

Elaeagnus angustifolia (oleaster) Deciduous shrub or small tree with silver willow-like leaves. Propagate

from semi-ripe cuttings. Plant in a well-drained soil in sun or shade.

Melianthus major The large pinnate fronds of this handsome small shrub have a curious chocolatey smell when bruised; an acquired taste for some. It is not hardy, so in cold climates must be overwintered under glass. In summer it has long, tapering racemes of glossy, bead-like flowers, but the foliage is the thing, and gives a distinctly tropical look in a border planting. Propagate from basal cuttings in late summer and plant in a well-drained soil in sun.

Cryptomeria japonica "Globosa Nana" *(above)* is just one of the several autumn-coloring evergreens this genus provides, contributing purple, bronze and dark red tints to the garden. *Picea pungens* "Koster Prostrate" *(below)* is, however, a dependable glaucous blue-gray, and the stiff finger-like branches give the shrub a fascinating visual texture.

Perovskia atriplicifolia (Russian sage) is one of the finest gray plants in the late summer garden with silvery-white stems covered in minuscule flowers making clouds of azure blue above the finely cut, ghostly pale foliage. "Blue Spire" and the lavender-tinted "Superba" are cultivars to look for. The scent is like sage with a hint of mothballs. Propagate this deciduous subshrub from semi-ripe cuttings in late summer and plant in a well-drained soil in sun.

Rosa rubrifolia has russet-red arching stems and red-tinged gray foliage against which the single flowers, colored pale rose madder, show up wonderfully. The flowers are followed by clusters of glossy ruby-red hips that last well into winter. Self-sown seedlings will appear, and it can also be increased from semi-ripe cuttings taken in summer. It makes a medium-sized shrub that will thrive in any soil in sun.

Salix lanata is called woolly willow on account of the exceptional caterpillar-like catkins that cover this low spreading shrub in spring. The stubby little round-ed leaves also have a silvery bloom. It roots easily from cuttings taken in late summer; give it a moisture-retentive soil in sun.

Salvia officinalis "Crispa" The leaves of this decorative form of common sage are more rounded than the species and the edges are crimped, causing the leaves to curl and crinkle. It makes a pleasing low-spreading gray mound. *S. o.* "Purpurascens" (purple-leaved sage) has a good inky tinge to the gray-green leaves. Propagate by cuttings in late summer. This hardy evergreen shrub prefers well-drained soil in sun.

Trees take their weeping habits from the depth of the angle where branch meets trunk, as can be seen in the weeping
Pyrus salicifolia (below). However, the drooping tassels of the needle clusters on the Bhutan pine, *Pinus wallichiana
(above)*, contribute the weeping effect to this graceful evergreen.

***Thymus* spp. and cultivars** are the
sweetest-smelling groundcovers. *T.
pseudolanuginosus*'s tiny leaves are
covered in fine silver hairs. To keep a
dense mat of foliage, clip the plants after
flowering. Increase from rooted pieces
lifted in autumn or spring; these mostly
hardy plants like well-drained soil in sun.

Trees

***Cryptomeria japonica* "Globosa Nana"**
A small evergreen shrub with a rounded
habit. The leaves turn bronze in winter.
Plant in a well-drained soil in sun or
partial shade. Propagate by semi-ripe
cuttings.

Picea pungens glauca The neat conical
habit and uniformly spaced spreading
branches of this glaucous evergreen
make a terrific feature in the garden but
it does need space to do it justice; if you
lack that, "Koster" or "Koster Prostrate"
are smaller-growing with the same coloring. Plant in a well-drained soil in sun
or semi-shade.

Pinus wallichiana (Bhutan pine) A
large evergreen tree with a weeping
appearance and long, graceful,
pendulous needles. Plant in a well-
drained soil in sun.

***Pyrus salicifolia* "Pendula"** is one of
the ornamental pears. A small tree, it is
grown for the graceful, willow-like silver
leaves and its pleasing weeping habit. It
benefits from selective pruning and
training to help it attain a good shape.
P. calleryana "Chanticleer" and *P. c.*
"Bradford" provide brilliant autumn
coloring in shades of purple and red
respectively. Plant in a well-drained soil
in sun.

BLUE-GREEN

The lady's mantle, *Alchemilla mollis*, is one of the garden's great all-arounders, grown for its elegant habit, foamy flower and seedheads, and the pinked leaf edges which capture each dew-drop to wear like a necklace of priceless gems.

The ice-blue tones of the hardy perennial grass *Elymus magellanicus (above left)* are repeated in the tender pink-tipped leaves of *Echeveria lindsayana (above right)* and the graceful concave leaves of *Dudleya brittonii (below)*. Such cool colors can be used to give a visual chill to sun-trap gardens.

Annuals and perennials

Alchemilla mollis This small perennial is beautiful from early summer when the fan-shaped leaves first open to late autumn when the blue-green hue fades to a khaki sprawl of seedheads, leaves and stems. It is easily propagated by division or from self-sown seedlings and will grow in any soil in sun (although in hot climates it does best in semi-shade).

Dudleya brittonii This is a perennial succulent with narrow lance-shaped pale blue leaves. Propagate by leaf cuttings. It is not frost-hardy; plant in a well-drained soil in sun.

Echeveria lindsayana A perennial succulent with rounded silvery blue-green leaves. Propagate by leaf cuttings. It is not hardy and needs a well-drained soil in sun.

Elymus magellanicus It is hard to think of a bluer grass, or plant for that matter. It makes an untidy tussock of limp leaves from which the erect flower stems emerge; they fade to a pleasing beige. Propagate by division at any time of year except winter. A herbaceous perennial, it will grow in any soil in sun.

Festuca glauca makes a spiky little hummock, about 12 in. (30 cm) around, of dark aqua-blue blades; use individuals as feature plants or spread in drifts in the front of taller-growing plants. It bears inconspicuous flowers on tall stems in early summer and is good on gravel or in containers. Remove dead foliage and faded flower stems. The variety *caesia* is a vivid electric blue. Propagate by division in spring. Plant this evergreen perennial in well-drained soil in sun.

Among the many hostas that have blue-green coloring, *H. sieboldiana* var. *elegans (left)* is one of the most desirable; the broad flat expanse of its waxy heart-shaped leaves makes an excellent foil to finer-textured foliage plants like the ground-hugging evergreen *Abies procera* "Glauca Prostrata" *(right)* which has a similar languid coloring.

Helictotrichon sempervirens Next to *Elymus*, this does stand out as one of the duck-eggiest blues in the plant world. It makes a nicely shaped spiky hummock, topped in midsummer by erect stems carrying arching panicles of flowers that fade to a satisfying sandy brown. Propagate by division in spring. Plant in dry soil in the sun and remove faded leaves and flower stems in early spring.

Hosta species and cultivars range in size from tiny groundcovers to clump-forming specimens with an eventual girth of 5 ft. (1.5 m), such as *Hosta sieboldiana* var. *elegans* which has huge deeply puckered silvery blue leaves. Other recommended blue cultivars are "Big Daddy" with nearly round cupped leaves of chalky glaucous blue and "Hadspen Blue" with heart-shaped, smooth, thick blue leaves. Use hostas in bold masses or as feature plants or grown in containers. Propagate by division. These herbaceous perennials, native to the forests of Japan and the Far East, appreciate dappled shade and moist soils, although some are tolerant of sun and dry spells, particularly in cool climates. Slugs and snails will disfigure the leaves.

Koeleria vallesiana This perennial grass does well on alkaline soil, making a mound of narrow blue-green leaves from which the erect flower stems emerge in midsummer. In all it grows to about 18 in. (45 cm). Divide in the spring. Any soil in sun will be acceptable.

Shrubs and climbers

Abies spp. *A. procera* "Glauca Prostrata" is a low bush with spreading branches and blue-green glaucous leaves. *A. concolor* "Compacta" (syn. *A. c.* "Glauca Compacta") is a small "blue" conifer with

Lacy-leaved rue is an excellent filler plant in the border among traditional perennials and old shrub roses; "Jackman's Blue" *(left)* has the best blue coloring, and there is also a cream variegated sort, "Variegata." Blue-green foliage is popular among flower arrangers for filling in between cut blooms, and *Eucalyptus cordata (right)* is highly favored by florists.

a graceful spreading habit and slow growth. It likes a moisture-retentive (preferably acid) soil in sun.

Ruta graveolens is the familiar shrubby herb commonly known as rue. On a sunny day the crushed leaves, which have an astringent pungency, can cause your skin to blister badly, so take care when clipping and tidying. "Jackman's Blue" has the best-colored glaucous blue-green foliage. Cut back hard each spring to keep shapely. Propagate by semi-ripe cuttings in summer and plant in well-drained soil in sun.

Trees

Eucalyptus **spp.** One of the most elegant compositions I have ever seen was a burned-out stand of acacia and eucalyptus trees regenerating, with the pastel tints of gray and pink from the gum trees and buttery yellow from the fragrant flowers of the acacia combining beautifully. *E. cordata* (silver gum) is a small tree with silver-gray leaves and an attractive white bark with green or purplish patches. *E. nicholii* (Nichol's willow-leaf peppermint gum) has purple-tinged leaves and a weeping form; *E. perriniana* is the

spinning gum, so called because the mature leaves break from the stem and then spin around it in the wind; *E. pulverulenta* has leaves powdered with gray "snow"; and *E. risdonii* (Risdon peppermint) has stems covered in a downy white bloom, as does *E. morrisbyi* (Morrisby's gum), which also has graceful lanceolate foliage. Seed from temperate zone parents will yield trees better adapted to cooler winter conditions than those raised from seed collected in Australia. Hard pruning will give the best foliage but will destroy the slender form. They require well-drained soil in sun.

YELLOW-VARIEGATED

Astrantia major "Sunningdale Variegated," with well-defined markings on its deeply lobed leaves, is one of the better herbaceous perennials valued for their foliage. However, as with many variegated hardy plants, the flowers have considerably less impact than the leaves.

Tender perennials, for example canna lilies, generally have vibrant flowers supported by equally stunning foliage. Orange-flowered *Canna* "Striata," with its broad oval leaves boldly striped in green and gold, is a popular plant, while the red-flowered "Lucifer" has dark burgundy-purple foliage.

Annuals and perennials

Astrantia major "**Sunningdale Variegated**" This clump-forming hardy perennial is strongly variegated and makes a good feature plant. Propagate by division in spring. Plant in any soil in sun or shade.

Canna "**Striata**" *A* tender perennial with flamboyant foliage, this plant requires a sunny position and a rich well-drained soil. In winter, store in damp peat away from frost. Propagate by division of rhizomes in spring.

Carex reticulosa "**Aurea**" Each blade of this vibrant perennial grass is like a ray of watery sunshine; *C. elata* "Bowles' Golden" is a deeper yellow, edged in emeralds; "Knightshayes" has the same radiance but without the green edging to each leaf. Propagate from division of rhizomatous roots or from seed and plant in moist soil in semi-shade.

Carex morrowii The bright bundles of variegated foliage are like spotlights in a garden scheme, highlighting interesting corners or illuminating dark ones. A perennial grass only about 6 in. (15 cm) tall, it is most easily increased by division in spring. It likes a moisture-retentive soil in semi-shade.

Hakonechloa macra is a distinctive little perennial grass increasing slowly by its rhizomatous roots to make thickets of arching leaves; there are several variegated cultivars, but the most vigorous and most often seen is "Aureola," which is very heavily yellow-variegated and showy. As winter approaches, the tips of the leaves become tinged brownish-red. Increase by division in spring and plant in moisture-retentive soil in semi-shade.

Vinca major "Variegata" *(left)* is a vigorous groundcovering evergreen excellent to use beneath trees and shrubs, but it is too strong for mixed perennial plantings, for which you could use *V. minor* "Variegata," a smaller, more refined version to partner spring flowers. *Elaeagnus × ebbengei* "Limelight" *(right)* is a reliable provider of winter interest.

***Molina caerulea* spp. *caerulea* "Variegata"** This popular perennial grass forms dense tussocks of creamy-white-variegated leaves; *M. c.* ssp. *arundinacea* "Bergfreund" has bright yellow autumn coloring; *M. c.* ssp. *arundinacea* "Windspiel" ("Windplay") should, as the name suggests, be planted where the breeze can put it in motion. It is easy to propagate by division in the spring. Plant in moisture-retentive soil in sun.

***Thymus* spp.** and cultivars include some of the best mat-forming yellow-variegated groundcovers, such as *T. caespititius* "Aureus" and *T. c.* "Doone Valley," which is particularly bold in its glossy little dark green leaves, heavily marked with yellow. It roots as it spreads so is very easy to propagate. Thyme is a hardy plant that likes well-drained soil in sun.

***Vinca major* "Variegata"** is the yellow-variegated form of the common periwinkle. This is an evergreen ground-cover that spreads by runners which root where they touch the ground. The leaves are glossy and heavily marked with yellow; used in a shady woodland setting it will look like pools of sunlight. Propagate from rooted runners. It will grow in any soil in sun or semi-shade.

Shrubs and climbers

***Elaeagnus* × *ebbengei* "Limelight"** This is a large evergreen shrub with a spreading habit. Its leathery green leaves have a central splash of gold or pale green. Alternatively the leaf margins of "Gilt Edge" are splashed with gold. Propagate from semi-ripe cuttings. Plant in a well-drained soil in sun.

Variegated evergreen plants make good focal points in the garden and also give permanence to planting schemes by carrying garden interest throughout the year. The evergreen plants shown here – climbing (or carpeting) *Hedera colchica* "Sulphur Heart" *(left)* and glittering *Ilex × altaclarensis* "Lawsoniana" *(right)* – both serve this purpose well.

***Hedera colchica* "Sulphur Heart"** has large heart-shaped leaves splashed with golden yellow. It is a good evergreen climber to use in dark corners of the garden, where it will bring a warm glow all year round. Occasionally a whole leaf will be yellow and on older leaves the yellow may have a greenish tone. Any soil in sun or semi-shade will suffice.

Hedera helix is a species of small-leaved evergreen ivy with a long list of cultivars, many of them variegated white or yellow. Of the latter, "Goldchild" is probably one of the best with its bright green leaves

splashed with pale green in the center surrounded by a golden yellow margin. Increase from layers or cuttings taken in late summer. It requires moisture-retentive soil in semi-shade.

***Ilex × altaclarensis* "Lawsoniana"** A large shrub or medium-sized tree with brightly colored large spineless leaves splashed with yellow in the center. Alternatively, *I. × a.* "Golden King" has broad green almost spineless leaves with a yellow margin and *I. × a.* "Belgica Aurea" has flat deep green leaves with a creamy yellow margin. Any soil in sun.

***Rosmarinus officinalis* "Aureus"** is the gilded rosemary treasured in the cottage and knot gardens and parterres of earlier centuries. Rosemary is generally a splendid evergreen shrub – there are prostrate forms, weeping forms and white- and pink-flowered cultivars, all smelling and tasting delicious – but the gold-splashed variegations of the gilded rosemary make it particularly special. It is not fully hardy, so give it a sheltered spot or else overwinter it under glass. Propagate from semi-ripe cuttings in summer. It requires a well-drained soil in sun.

WHITE-VARIEGATED

White variegation appears less showy than yellow; perhaps because it blends more easily with the soft pastel shades of spring and early summer. *Arum italicum* "Marmoratum" appears as the first bulbs begin to push through.

Ornamental brassicas make a terrific annual display for the winter garden and the F1 hybrid mixes offered by seed merchants give you selections of ruff-leaved cabbages and spider-lace kale in shades of pink, carmine, and most spectacularly, white.

Annuals and perennials

***Arum italicum* "Marmoratum"** (lords and ladies) When most other foliage plants are losing their glamour in autumn this herbaceous perennial begins to put on a show, sending up large, glossy, arrowhead-shaped leaves deeply veined in silvery white. Use with hellebores and other winter- and early spring-flowering plants. Propagate by division after the leaves have faded away or just as they begin to emerge. There will be plenty of self-sown seedlings as well to increase your stock.

Plant in moisture-retentive soil in sun or semi-shade.

***Arundo donax* "Variegata"** (syn. *A. d.* var. *versicolor*) For a bold exclamation point this stately perennial grass can hardly be bettered. Erect stems well above the height of the average adult carry narrow strappy leaves variegated in bold white stripes. It is not hardy so must be overwintered under glass, but is well worth the effort. An essential ingredient of the tropical border. Site in moisture-retentive soil in sun and propagate by division in spring.

Brassica oleracea provides gardeners with ornamental cabbage and kale as well as nourishing "greens." Most seed catalogues now list these frilly fancies, with shades of creamy white, pink, and mauve brightening the crunchy leaves. Grow as for winter cabbages, then plant out into the garden or, best of all, fill containers with bouquets of them. Sow the seed in early summer in a seedbed and then prick out into individual pots. Pot on as the plants develop and feed well to achieve really spectacular plants. They will thrive in any soil. Added lime benefits growth.

In some foliage plants, the variegation emphasizes the shape or structure of the leaves; the curves and undulations of *Hosta undulata* var. *univittata (above)* are enhanced by the bold splash of white variegation, just as the slender leaves of *Miscanthus sinensis* "Malepartus" *(opposite above)* look even skinnier because of the single white central stripe. Some variegation, however, will simply frost each leaf with silver, as in the annual *Lunaria annua* "Alba Variegata" *(opposite below)*.

Carex spp. *C. oshimensis* grows to about 12 in. (30 cm) and has much broader leaves than other *Carex* species. It has an equally bright variegation with each leaf boldly edged in white; the form "Evergold" is edged in clotted-cream yellow. When this perennial grass is planted in large groups the variegation creates a shimmering effect like light on the surface of the sea. *Carex siderosticha* "Variegata" is a stunning specimen plant with broad white-variegated leaves; it makes a graceful mound composed of long ribbon-like leaves, each one clearly edged in white. It is a perennial plant which grows to about 18 in. (45 cm). Propagate by division in the spring and plant in a moisture-retentive soil in sun or semi-shade.

Hosta undulata* var. *univittata This is a hardy perennial with undulate leaves carrying a central white stripe of variegation. Over the years the plant becomes less variegated eventually reverting to green. Propagate by division. Plant in shade in a rich moisture-retentive soil.

Lunaria annua "Alba Variegata" (honesty) A quick-growing biennial with variegated coarse-toothed, heart-shaped leaves. Propagate by seed. Plant in a well-drained soil in semi-shade.

Miscanthus sinensis I have picked this particular species of *Miscanthus* because it gives the most choice of garden varieties and is easy to grow. It also offers some good specimen plants for the border or garden when you need something other than a shrub and the flowers are quite showy for a grass, in some varieties appearing quite late in the autumn. The broad leaves of "Malepartus" are enhanced by a thin white central stripe

Phalaris arundinacea "Picta" *(left)*, better known as gardener's garters, is flashier than many white-variegated plants, but is incredibly invasive, especially in moisture-retentive soils; the sort known as "Feesey's Form" is less troublesome and has even stronger, whiter markings.

while "Silberfeder" (or "Silverfeather") grows to at least 8 ft. (2.4 m) when well suited and is topped with gloriously silky flowerheads that glisten in the breeze of a sunny autumn day. "Variegatus" is widely available, with leaves having a broad white stripe variegation; "Zebrinus" is cream variegated with horizontal stripes across the leaf blade rather than along it. "Morning Light" has the silvery effect of "Silberfeder" enhanced by a broad white stripe along the leaf margins. Propagate by division in spring. Give it moisture-retentive soil in sun or semi-shade.

***Persicaria virginiana* "Painter's Palette"** *(syn. Tovara virginiana* "Painter's Palette") is a low-growing hardy perennial forming loose mounds of oval mid-green foliage splashed with cream and marked with a garnet-red chevron across each leaf. This color is echoed on the stems, giving the plant a rather reddish cast. Plant in moisture-retentive soil in sun and propagate by division.

***Phalaris arundinacea* "Picta"** is a perennial grass with broad white-striped leaves which taper to a point. This plant

can be invasive. Propagate by division. Plant in any soil in the sun.

***Pulmonaria* spp. and cultivars** (lung-wort) There are dozens of species and named cultivars of this familiar cottage garden herb bearing varying degrees of silvery markings on long, tapering leaves with a slightly rough texture. *P. rubra* "David Ward" has soft gray-green coloring and bold creamy-white variegation; *P. longifolia* "Bertram Anderson" has long narrow leaves and glittering spots of silver that are especially bright in autumn; and *P. saccharata*

The heavily variegated oval leaves of the lungwort *Pulmonaria saccharata* Argentea Group *(center)* are at their best in spring. Splashed with varying degrees of silver, they are a perfect foil for spring flower color among hellebores, narcissus, and primroses. The white markings of the climber *Actinida kolomikta (right)* are tinged with sunburn pink; always buy a plant in leaf to be sure of having good variegation – some plants perform better than others.

Argentea Group has heavily silvered leaves mottled with dark gray-green. Pulmonarias are supremely collectible, and are good clump-formers to use as ground cover among spring-flowering plants, hellebores, and heucheras. Propagate by division in autumn. They like moisture-retentive soil in semi-shade.

Shrubs and climbers

Actinidia kolomikta is a vigorous twining climber with broad, vaguely heart-shaped deciduous leaves that are splashed at the tips with white and pink; sometimes the entire leaf will show little evidence of green. However, plants will not show variegation until mature. Small fragrant white flowers open in early summer. This climber can be propagated by layering or internodal cuttings and will grow in any soil in full sun.

Hedera colchica **"Dentata Variegata"** is an evergreen ivy with large heart-shaped leaves edged in creamy white. Use it to clothe fences and cover walls or as groundcover to create a bright carpet for spring bulbs to show through; it will grow in any soil in sun or semi-shade.

Trees

Cornus controversa **"Variegata"** It is worth spending a little extra to obtain the best specimen you can of this splendid tree and then give it the best treatment you can. The reward will be a stunning display of tiered branches covered in bright silvery variegation. Let it be one of the stars of the garden by giving it a place center stage. In autumn the leaves often turn a rich purple-red. A medium-sized deciduous tree, it likes well-drained soil in sun or semi-shade.

AUTUMN COLOR

The rusty leaves of the sedge *Carex comans* bronze are a curious mix of khaki-green and brick-red. As the seasons pass the leaves fade from their tips to a warm biscuit brown in autumn and retain this soft coloring throughout winter.

Euphorbias provide gardeners with a huge range of color, texture, form, and habit from which to choose. There are tiny-leaved wine-red sorts and others with bright green needle-like leaves. Some have erect stems, while there are many lax, mound-forming varieties. They contribute to the scene all year round, but autumn particularly benefits, especially from *Euphorbia griffithii* "Fireglow."

Annuals and perennials

***Carex* spp.** There are nearly 2000 species of this sedge and among them are some stunning perennial foliage plants providing shades of cinnamon brown, brassy green, and bright yellow and white variegations. Although they retain their color all year round it is of particular value in autumn when most perennials are past their best.
C. buchananii is erect, growing to about 2 ft. (60 cm), and has glossy copper foliage that can make sudden loose corkscrew curls at the tips; *C. comans*

bronze only grows to about 10 in. (25 cm) and makes a soft spreading tuft of rather glossy leaves tinted pale cordovan brown – outstanding planted in ribbons through a border. Propagate by division in spring and place in moisture-retentive soil in sun or semi-shade.

***Euphorbia* spp and cultivars** This genus of evergreen perennials provides some of the finest "feature" plants in the garden – the sort of plant you place in eye-catching positions or else use as markers in the scheme of things. While they look good for most of the year, I

think they really come into their own in the autumn. They are available in a wide range of sizes, from the small ground-covering *E. cyparissias* with short, limp stems covered in pale green leaves resembling bottle brushes to the large and widely grown *E. characias* ssp. *wulfenii*, which has erect stems covered in glaucous blue-green narrow leaves topped by whorls of lime-green flower bracts. In between, *E. × martinii* has a similar habit of upright growth but red-tinged stems and leaves. Other red euphorbias are *E. griffithii* "Dixter," which has a particularly dense color,

An uncommon member of the ubiquitous cotoneaster clan is *Cotoneaster lancasterii (left)*, seen here at Saling Hall in Essex, England. The mix of fiery red, gold, and silver-backed leaves makes this a splendid shrub for the autumn border. Plants of the Monticola Group of *Fothergilla major (center)* have the characteristic white bottle-brush flowers on naked stems, but only after the shrub has shed its glorious fireflame autumn raiment.

E. g. "Fireglow," and *E. dulcis* "Chameleon," which is almost entirely dark burgundy red, with the hint of green about it equally murky. It makes a good clump of foliage among spring-flowering plants. *E. seguieriana* ssp. *niciciana* has arching stems of stubby blue-gray leaves. Propagate from cuttings in late summer or else by division (or self-sown seedlings in the case of *E. dulcis* "Chameleon"). They require well-drained soil in sun or semi-shade.

Geranium macrorrhizum "Album" is the white-flowered cultivar of this hardy geranium which is best loved for the resin-scented foliage that takes on rust-red and purple tones during autumn. It is easily propagated by cuttings taken throughout summer or by division and will grow in any soil in sun.

Shrubs and climbers

Cotoneaster lancasterii Most members of this genus have something to offer but for bold autumn color, this species is worth searching for. Propagate by semi-ripe cuttings. Plant in any soil in sun or part shade.

Fothergilla (witch alder) *F. gardenii* makes a rounded mound of soft blue-green foliage that turns fiery orange in autumn; in spring the naked branches bear dense clusters of scented white flowers. *F. g.* "Blue Mist" is a widely available cultivar that colors well and *F. major* makes an upright shrub bearing fluffy white scented flowers on naked branches during mid- to late spring. The serrate oval leaves are a rather dull gray-green, turning to excellent shades of gold and scarlet in autumn. Propagate from semi-ripe cuttings in late summer. These

Parthenocissus tricuspidata (right), better known as Boston ivy, is the mournful cladding of many a late-nineteenth-century building, shrouding every architectural detail in a mantle of flat green. However, the autumn color can be spectacular; "Veitchii" becomes dark burgundy purple and "Lowii" has deeply cut and frilled edges.

medium-sized deciduous shrubs do best on acid moisture-retentive soil in semi-shade.

Hamamelis mollis is the witch hazel, a deciduous large shrub or small tree which is beautiful all year round. In early spring the branches are alive with delicately perfumed flowers which are replaced by heavily textured, broad, rounded leaves that turn golden yellow in autumn. The habit is broad and spreading and the plant matures slowly. It prefers acid soil but will grow in any good well-drained soil in semi-shade.

Parthenocissus quinquefolia (Virginia creeper), although more widely grown, is less interesting than *P. henryana*, whose leaves have three to five leaflets with a soft matte surface veined in palest pink or white. The veins remain prominent even when the foliage has taken on the rich ruby tints of autumn. *P. tricuspidata* has a shorter moment of autumn glory when its broad-lobed and glossy surfaced leaves turn a startling ruby-red color; unfortunately for much of the rest of the year it can lack interest. Initially, all climb by tendrils, so walls should be fixed with wires; they

can also be used to clothe dull trees and brighten east- or north-facing aspects. Propagate from soft cuttings in summer. They like well-drained soil in full or semi-shade.

Viburnum spp. and cultivars provide the autumn and early spring garden with some good color and textures; there are deciduous and evergreen sorts to choose from. *V. davidii* has dark green, slightly glossy, but heavily veined leaves, giving it a rough-looking texture; it makes a low, spreading evergreen shrub and there are male and female

Vitis coignetiae needs plenty of space since it has the largest leaves of any of the grape vines. Huge, heart-shaped and coloring splendidly in late autumn, they are particularly useful for clothing walls that are north-facing since this vine will grow there as happily as in full sun.

plants so to have the steel-blue berries you must grow one of each. *V. rhytidophyllum* is a large rounded evergreen shrub that has long, tapering leaves, deep green in color on the top and a bland gray-green beneath. The corymbs of small white flowers are followed by glossy red then black fruits. It has a way of looking extremely sorry for itself in cold weather, when the leaves take on a pronounced downward droop – not to everyone's liking. *V. sargentii* "Onondaga" has vinous-red deciduous leaves that shade through deep green back to red again as they

age; the stems and flowers also have a pleasing red tinge as though dipped in aged port. *V. plicatum* "Mariesii," *V. p. tomentosum*, and *V. p.* "Watanabe" all have an extremely elegant tiered habit of growth with branches growing like outstretched arms. The flowers appear along the tops of the branches and the deeply textured deciduous leaves curve gracefully downwards so that the shrubs look like southern belles in crinolines. In autumn the leaves are tinged with pink and red. *V. opulus* "Aureum" is the yellow-leaved form of the common guelder rose and makes a bright splash in spring

when the leaves first open. Propagate from cuttings in late summer. These are medium-sized shrubs that like moisture-retentive soil in semi-shade.

Vitis spp. and cultivars If you have ever seen an ordinary grape vine coloring up as the grapes ripen you will know the potential of this genus. Among the most spectacular climbers for autumn color is *V. coignetiae*, with its huge heart-shaped leaves that begin to take on the luscious tints of Florentine silks as the first frosts approach. Gradually the whole plant becomes

The palmate group of Japanese maples, species and varieties and forms within *Acer palmatum*, offer the garden-maker a widely varying selection of cultivars from which to choose. The autumn coloring effects are beautiful, many of them have attractive bark and, in some instances, the seedpods are also brightly colored.

garnet red, and then the leaves begin to drop one by one. It is a vigorous vine and so needs room to spread – or else stern control with pruners. It is good on a north-facing wall. Another grape for autumn color is *V.* "Brant" which has soft green leaves in youth that color red between the veins as the weather chills, giving a pleasing mottled effect. *V.* "Purpurea" is the purple-leaved grape vine and *V.* "Incana" is the gray-leaved Dusty Miller grape, the foliage of which looks as though it has been dusted over with flour. All of these can be propagated from cuttings in late summer.

They are deciduous climbers that like well-drained soil in sun or part shade.

Trees

Acer There are dozens of maples I could suggest for autumn color but my list would have to start with *A. saccharum*, the sugar maple famous for the colors of the New England fall. It is a tall-growing tree, at its best when planted in groves to make the most of the widely varying warm hues of the foliage. *A. saccharinum* is the silver maple, so called because the backs of the leaves

have a silvery sheen that gives the tree a shimmering glow when the wind stirs the branches; the form *A. s.* f. *laciniatum* has elegant, deeply cut leaves carried on loose drooping branches. *A. palmatum* "Osakazuki" is also renowned for the brilliance of its fiery scarlet leaves in autumn. These fairly fast-growing small to medium deciduous trees will thrive in any soil in sun.

Koelreuteria paniculata This tree is worth having for the common name alone: golden rain tree, probably so called for the marvelous autumn color

Often mistaken for a maple because of its palmate leaves, *Liquidambar styraciflua (above)* also shares the brilliant autumn coloring – sometimes. Trees raised from cuttings of the clones "Worplesdon" or "Lane Roberts" are, however, sure-fire selections. The young growth of *Nyssa sinensis (below)* anticipates the bright red coloring of its autumn foliage.

of the pinnate foliage which makes the broad spreading tree look like a cloud of golden raindrops. It carries panicles of yellow flowers that turn to bladder-like fruit in late summer. A medium-sized deciduous tree, it will grow in any soil in sun. The cultivar "Fastigiata" is a small tree with a tidy columnar habit.

Liquidambar styraciflua (sweet gum) This deciduous tree of medium size provides the most glorious autumn colors, from deep burgundy purple leaves on the lowest branches to sun-burst yellow in the uppermost, or else

solidly wine red – it all depends on the tree and the soil, it seems. In my garden the young tree stayed a lackluster browny green in its first few autumns, but now, eight years on, it gives me the most profound pleasure with lovely lingering ruby-red palmate leaves and an elegant conical habit. It requires moisture-retentive soils in sun or semi-shade and will not tolerate shallow alkaline soils.

Nothofagus fusca (red beech) has glorious coppery tints in the autumn and on older trees the bark develops a flaking appearance. *N. solandri* (black

beech) is valued for the graceful way the tiny leaves gather in fan-like clusters on the wiry stems; *N. s.* var. *cliffortioides* is most easily available. Both of these small trees are New Zealand natives and are quite hardy, but appreciate shelter from strong winds. They require well-drained acid soil in sun or semi-shade.

Nyssa spp. The glossy dark green foliage of *N. sylvatica*,the black gum or tupelo tree, gives spectacular blazing autumn color. This medium-sized tree has a pleasing broad columnar habit, making it a good specimen tree for a

In early spring the young leaves of *Prunus sargentii* are a soft coppery red that offsets the pale pink flowers perfectly.
It makes a graceful tree with its broad spreading crown and, come early autumn, the foliage turns a deep crimson,
heralding the change of the season.

distant view. It is fairly slow-growing so it takes a while to come into its own, and since it dislikes being transplanted it is best to buy a young tree. *N. sinensis* has narrowish leaves which change to a vibrant blend of vivid reds in autumn. Give them a moist soil in sun.

Parrotia persica (Persian ironwood) is a broadly spreading small deciduous tree with exceptionally hard wood. It is a relative of the witch hazel and shares that tree's graceful habit. In autumn, the long oval leaves color golden yellow, touched with apple red at the tips. They

are quite slow-growing but a mature tree is a beautiful thing, especially when complemented by autumn-flowering *Cyclamen hederifolium*. It requires moisture-retentive soil in sun.

Populus tremuloides (quaking aspen) Like the bamboo *(see page 148)* this is a garden music-maker as the fluttering leaves create movement and sound in an open setting. The foliage colors a radiant golden yellow. This deciduous tree can grow to 100 ft. (30 m), so it needs space and perspective to be appreciated. It prefers well-drained soil in sun.

Prunus sargentii (Sargent's cherry) has long, tapering oval leaves and a broad, upright, spreading crown. In spring there are pretty clusters of shell-pink flowers; during the summer the tree is simply green and leafy, but come autumn the foliage is among the first to turn gradually to shades of vermilion, ochre, chrome yellow, and palest buttercup. This lasts for a few magnificent days, then the leaves drop all at once to the ground – still looking splendid. A small deciduous tree, it likes well-drained soil in sun and is good in alkaline soils.

BARK, STEM, & BERRY

Chusquea culeou is one of the most stately bamboos, referred to by one specialist grower as "the cream of bamboos."
The beautifully banded canes alone make it worth growing, with the arching sprays of fine foliage providing a perfect
counterpoint to its demanding visual presence.

Eryngium bourgatii "Oxford Blue" is spectacular for its icy stem coloring that creeps into the bracts and seedheads.
The old Edwardian favorite *E.* × *zabelii* is a hybrid of lavishly ruffed *E. alpinum* and *E. bourgatii*, so it has the lacy
bracts of the first and the rich coloring of the latter.

Annuals andN perennials

Briza maxima is commonly known as
quaking grass because the delightful
pendent spikelets dip and bob in the
breeze; the inflorescence appears
throughout summer followed by seedheads which turn a soft buff straw color
as they dry. An annual, it self-seeds
freely. Divide in spring to increase
stocks. *Briza* will grow in any soil in sun
or semi-shade.

Chasmanthium latifolium has the most
graceful inflorescence of any grass,
bearing panicles of thumbnail-sized
flowers that look like flattened outsize
oats dangling from the finest of stems.
It is erect-growing to about 3 ft. (90 cm),
with drooping leaves widely spaced
along the length of each stem. Place it
where the movement of the panicles,
which fade from pale green to biscuit
brown, can be easily observed.
Propagate by division in spring. It
requires well-drained soil in semi-shade.

Chusquea culeou (Chilean bamboo)
is one of the best bamboos; it is very
hardy, very large with canes up to 15 ft.
(5 m) tall and forms dense clumps up to
10 ft. (3 m) across.

Eryngium bourgatii **"Oxford Blue"**
Tall multi-headed stems rise from a
ground-hugging rosette of deeply cut
and veined leaves. A metallic silver-blue
sheen dominates the leaves, stem, and
teasel-like flowerheads. Propagate this
perennial by division in the spring. Plant
in a well-drained soil in a sunny position.

Eupatorium purpureum (Joe Pye weed)
is a stately perennial with rather
uninteresting whorls of foliage wrapped

The silvered canes of *Rubus cockburnianus (left)* make a bold statement in the winter garden when contrasted against dark evergreens or among spring-flowering hellebores. The crimson bark of *Cornus alba* "Sibirica" *(center)* has a similarly startling effect, so the winter garden need not lack color interest.

around exceedingly tall erect red stems that are topped by umbels of rosy-red tubular flowers in late summer and early autumn. It grows to 6½ft. (2 m) or more. Propagate by division in autumn or early spring and plant in well-drained soil in semi-shade.

Hordeum jubatum Squirrel or fox-tail barley is an annual or short-lived perennial grass often seen growing wild in roadside verges or in field margins, singled out from the crowd by the gracefully arching stems carrying long feathery flower spikes that fade to

attractive seedheads. It will grow in any well-drained soil in sun.

Pennisetum **spp. and cultivars** This grass is valuable for the wonderful fluffy seedheads rather than for the loose tufts of limp foliage it produces. *P. alopecuroides* sends up arching flower stems in late summer that gradually transform into long panicles of seeds, each one tufted with long hairs, so that the plant looks as if it is covered in fuzzy caterpillars. *P. orientale* is much more glamorous, with a longer panicle and softer, silkier, pink-tinged hairs on

the seeds. *P. setaceum* is worth seeking out for the red-tinged color of the entire plant. Propagate from seed or by division in spring. Pennisetums prefer light, warm soils in sun.

Phyllostachys **spp. and cultivars** (bamboo) If you have no readily available source of water, I advise a group of bamboo placed where the breeze will stir its leaves; the soft rustle is as pleasing as any water feature. There are quite a number of *Phyllostachys* species, some of which have distinctly colorful and curiously shaped stems that can add

Cornus stolonifera "Flaviramea" *(right)* joins the other dogwoods in providing a vivacious color during the dull winter months. The finest hue on all such shrubs appears on new wood, so it is important to cut out old growth each spring to encourage new shoots for winter interest.

verticality to a planting scheme. *P. aurea* "Flavescens Inversa" carries a yellow groove along the internodal segments of the sturdy green stems, or culms, while *P. bambusoides* "Castilloni" has green grooves on straw-yellow culms; *P. nigra* has brownish-black culms, and *P. n.* "Boryana" displays splashes of inky brown along them. *P. violascens* acquires purplish-green markings as it ages. Apply a mulch of well-rotted compost annually to help conserve moisture and occasionally thin out old stems to allow warm summer sun to penetrate to their hearts.

Propagate by division of the clumps. These evergreen perennials like moisture-retentive soil in sun or semi-shade.

Rubus **spp.** Recommended are *R. cockburnianus* with blue-white stems in winter, *R. phoenicolasius* (Japanese wineberry), with ruby-red heavily prickled stems and bright green leaves with silvered undersides, and *R. thibetanus*, much the most refined member of the family, with silvery feathery foliage and long, arching, waxy-white stems. Like all brambles they do run about, but are easily controlled by chopping out chunks.

They are hardy perennials that will thrive in any soil in sun.

Shrubs and climbers

Cornus **spp** *C. alba* (red-stem dogwood) is a vigorous medium-sized deciduous shrub with an upright habit, spreading into a rounded shape with age. The simple oval-shaped foliage colors well and brightly colored bark enhances young stems during winter. Shrubs grown for this effect should be positioned in full sun and cut back hard in spring. "Aurea" has soft yellow foliage;

The tidy linear structure of *Cotoneaster horizontalis (above)* is emphasized by the tiny crimson berries snug amid diminutive leaves; this plant makes excellent wall cover or groundcover beneath shrubs and hedges. *Pyracantha* "Orange Glow" *(below left)* is widely grown as a wall-trained shrub, covered in spring with clusters of white flowers, replaced by orange berries in autumn. *Rosa rugosa* "Scabrosa" *(below right)* is another suckering shrub with bright fruit and also autumn coloring; it provides good hedging in difficult conditions, like seaside gardens and dry shade.

in "Elegantissima" the soft green leaves are mottled and edged with white; "Kesselringii" has dark green leaves deepening to claret red in autumn on dark purple stems; "Sibirica" has fiery crimson stems in winter; and "Spaethii" has leaves variegated yellow. *Cornus stolonifera* "Flaviramea" has bright green-yellow bark in winter. Propagate from semi-ripe cuttings in late summer and plant in moisture-retentive to moist soil in sun or semi-shade.

Corylus avellana "Contorta" This medium-sized deciduous shrub really

only comes into its own in late maturity when it has the substance and height to carry off the oddly twisted branches and stems. The leaves carry the same distortion, so it looks unruly until leaf-drop, but bare stems and catkins together make a remarkable show. Propagate from semi-ripe cuttings taken in late summer. It will grow in any soil in sun or semi-shade.

Cotoneaster spp. There are dozens of cotoneasters and most are valued for their colorful berries in shades of red, orange, and yellow. Some species

(*C. horizontalis* in particular) will self-sow. Ranked according to leaf size, large to small, species and forms worth looking out for are: *C. bullatus, C. frigidus* "Cornubia," *C. dammeri, C. frigidus, C. salicifolius* "Rothschildianus," *C. × watereri* "John Waterer," *C. conspicuus* "Decorus," *C. horizontalis, C. microphyllus,* and *C. nitidus*. Propagate from semi-ripe cuttings in late summer. These medium to groundcovering shrubs will grow in any soil in sun or semi-shade.

Pyracantha spp. and cultivars (firethorn) These evergreen shrubs are

Symphoricarpos albus is aptly known as the snowberry; it is a common shrub that can make a suckering thicket so is often used as boundary hedge in its native North America.

most often grown as wall-trained specimens. Despite their pleasing tiny glossy leaves it is their berries which make them noteworthy, coming in shades of red, orange and yellow. *P.* "Orange Glow" and *P.* "Golden Charmer" describe themselves; *P.* "Watereri" has a compact habit and bright red fruit; *P. rogersiana* "Flava" has narrow dull green leaves but vibrant yellow berries; *P. atalantioides* has large glossy leaves and long-lasting clusters of bright red berries. Increase from cuttings taken in late summer and plant in well-drained soil in sun or semi-shade.

***Rosa* spp. and cultivars** A good many roses provide interesting stems and/or good autumn color from leaves and hips. The latter can be as round as golf balls or long and tapering like little bottles. *R. rugosa* "Scabrosa" comes to mind for its exceptional large, glowing red globes of seed-filled hips. In early autumn this is a marvelous spectacle with golden leaves, red hips, and spicily perfumed bright pink flowers appearing all at once. *R.* "Blanche Double de Coubert" makes a tall leggy shrub if left to itself, and in autumn the branches are covered in butter-yellow leaves that last well into

early winter. *R. foliolosa* makes a lax shrub with red-tinged stems and a dressing of pinnate leaves. It also has clusters of rusty-red hips. *R. californica* "Plena" makes an upright spreading shrub covered in clusters of starry flowers followed by masses of crimson hips amid the yellowing leaves. Provide with a well-drained soil and a sunny position.

Symphoricarpos albus A deciduous shrub bearing white to pink berries in autumn and winter. Plant in any well-drained soil in sun or shade. Propagate by division of suckers.

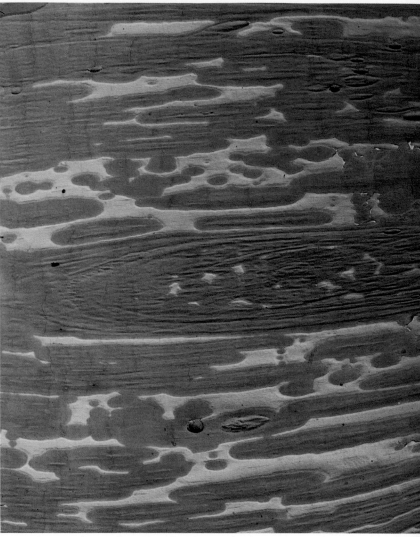

Specimen trees can be chosen for many reasons, and bark quality and character are high on the list. Many maples have good texture and color, like *Acer forestii* "Alice" *(left)* with its corrugated cordovan-colored bark. Birch, too, is well-loved as a feature tree, and *Betula ermanii (right)* displays the blotched whiteness characteristic of these trees.

Trees

Acer spp. *A. forestii* "Alice" is a small deciduous tree with striated bark which when young is a pretty coral-red. *A. griseum* is the paperbark maple, so called for its ginger-red peeling bark; plant it where the light will shine through the papery film. *A. capillipes* (snakebark maple) has a trunk marked with silvery-green striations. These deciduous trees thrive in any soil in sun or semi-shade.

Arbutus unedo This is known commonly as the strawberry tree on account of the bright red glossy fruit which, sadly, has no taste. Mature trees have superb Titian-red bark, smooth and pleasingly tactile, and glossy green foliage, making this a perfect medium-sized evergreen specimen tree. Give it shelter in cold gardens or raise it in a large tub. It requires well-drained soil in sun.

Betula pendula "Youngii," *B. jacque-montii* and *B. ermanii* "Grayswood Hill" are best for ghostly white bark effects. These are medium-sized deciduous trees and a group of them artfully placed to catch the setting sun is one of the great visual pleasures. Often the foliage will turn a pleasing buttery yellow in autumn. Place them in any soil in sun.

Calocedrus decurrens The incense cedar is one of the best trees for providing a vertical accent; the fan-shaped fronds fold themselves around the trunk, which is sheathed in pleasing scented red-tinged bark. It makes a large evergreen tree and will grow in any soil in sun.

Eucalyptus spp. These are fast-growing evergreen trees with lush foliage and attractive stems and trunks *(see page*

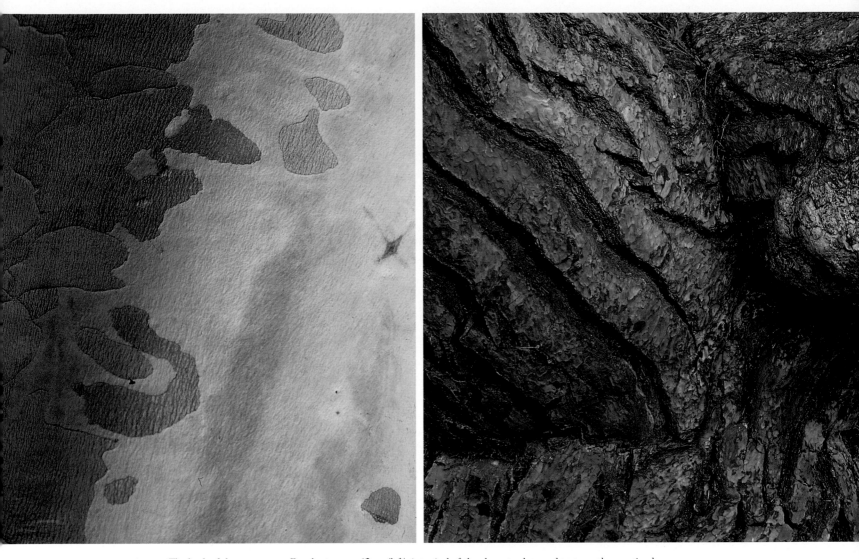

The bark of the snow gum, *Eucalyptus pauciflora (left)*, is typical of the elegant colors and textures these antipodean natives share; combined with the gray-green foliage they have a pale spectral presence in the garden unlike the rugged stone pine, *Pinus pinea (right)*, with its bold outline and heavily modeled bark textures.

127). *E. pauciflora* (snow gum) has a lovely snakeskin bark of green, gray, and cream. *E. johnstonii* (yellow gum) is a large tree with reddish bark. Avoid shallow soil over lime and plant in a sheltered position in sun or semi-shade.

Pinus spp. *P. pinea* (stone pine or umbrella pine) is a distinct medium-sized tree with a flat-topped head and reddish bark. *P. densiflora* "Umbraculifera" is the most interesting cultivar of the Japanese red pine. It grows only to about 10 ft. (3 m) but will eventually make a gracefully shaped dome

spreading to twice that size. The branches are dark and sinuous, giving the tree a distinctive shape rather like that seen on blue willow pattern china. *P. bungeana* (lacebark pine) is a large shrub or small tree which has a pale gray-green bark that flakes to create a camouflage effect. These evergreens will grow in any soil in sun or semi-shade.

Prunus spp. *P. serrula* is noted for its shiny peeling oxblood-red bark. In my garden I encourage visitors to strip off the bark to reveal the glossy new layers underneath. It will grow in any soil in

sun and is good in alkaline soils. *Prunus* "Taihaku" is also known as the great white cherry, much loved by Vita Sackville-West. There are few cherries which give a more breathtaking show; in early spring the foliage begins to appear as little bright green wings tinged with cherry red, followed by pendent clusters of pure white flowers. It makes a broad, upright spreading crown in maturity, but even the young trees have a pleasing outline. In autumn the foliage colors a lingering rust-red and gold. A medium-sized deciduous tree, it will grow in any soil in sun and is good in alkaline soils.

Plant site list

A guide to the siting of Plant Directory plants. Some entries may appear in more than one category.

Moisture-retentive soil in sun

Abies spp.
Acer palmatum and vars.
Arundo donax "Variegata"
Carex spp.
Cercis canadensis
Cornus spp.
Cotinus spp.
Gunnera manicata
Houttuynia cordata "Chameleon"
Liquidambar styraciflua
Lysichiton camtschatcensis
Miscanthus sinensis
Molina caerula ssp. *caerula* "Variegata"
Musa basjoo and *M. acuminata*
Nyssa sylvatica
Parrotia persica
Persicaria virginiana "Painter's Palette"
Phyllostachys spp. and cultivars
Ricinus communis
Rodgersia podophylla
Salix lanata
Zantedeschia aethiopica "Crowborough"

Moisture-retentive soil in shade or semi-shade

Adiantum venustum
Ajuga reptans
Arum italicum "Marmoratum"
Astilboides tabularis
Asplenium scolopendrium
Athyrium niponicum var. *pictum*
Carex spp.
Cornus spp.
Dicksonia antarctica
Filipendula ulmaria "Aurea"
Fothergilla spp.
Gunnera manicata
Hakonechloa macra
Hedera helix vars.
Hosta spp. and cultivars
Houttuynia cordata "Chameleon"
Hydrangea sargentiana
Liquidambar styraciflua
Lysichiton camtschatcensis and *L.* americanus
Lysimachia nummularia "Aurea"
Matteuccia struthiopteris
Milium effusum "Aureum"
Miscanthus sinensis
Phyllostachys spp. and cultivars
Polystichum setiferum
Pulmonaria spp. and cultivars
Veratrum nigrum
Viburnum spp. and cultivars
Zantedeschia aethiopica "Crowborough"

Well-drained soil in sun

Acanthus spp.
Agave spp.
Arbutus unedo
Artemisia ludoviciana "Silver Queen"
Aruncus dioicus "Kneiffii"
Berberis thunbergii "Red Pillar"
Canna musifolia "Striata"
Cordyline australis
Cornus controversa "Variegata"
Cryptomeria japonica "Globosa Nana"
Cupressus sempervirens
Cynara cardunculus
Dudleya brittonii
Echeveria lindsayana
Elaeagnus angustifolia and *E.* x *ebbengei* "Limelight"
Eryngium bourgatii "Oxford Blue"
Eucalyptus spp.
Euphorbia spp. and cultivars
Festuca glauca
Ficus carica
Geranium sessiliflorum "Nigricans"
Gleditsia triacanthos
Helictotrichon sempervirens
Helleborus x *sternii*
Hordeum jubatum
Juniperus spp.
Magnolia grandiflora
Melianthus major
Nandina domestica vars.
Nothofagus fusca
Ophiopogon planiscapus "Nigrescens"
Origanum vulgare "Aureum"
Pennisetum spp. and cultivars
Perilla frutescens
Perovskia atriplicifolia
Phormium tenax Purpureum Group

Acer palmatum "Dissectum Atropurpureum"

Dicksonia antarctica

Stachys byzantina

Picea pungens glauca

Pinus wallichiana

Populus tremuloides

Prunus cerasifera "Pissardii"

Prunus lusitanica

Prunus sargentii

Pyracantha spp. and cultivars

Pyrus salicifolia "Pendula"

Quercus spp. and cultivars

Rosa spp. and cultivars

Rosmarinus officinalis "Aureus"

Ruta graveolens

Salvia officinalis and cultivars

Sedum spp.

Stachys byzantina

Stipa spp.

Symphoricarpos albus

Thymus spp. and cultivars

Trachycarpus fortunei

Verbascum olympicum

Vitis spp. and cultivars

Well-drained soil in shade or semi-shade

Acanthus spp.

Aruncus dioicus "Kneiffii"

Berberis thunbergii "Red Pillar"

Chasmanthium latifolium

Cornus controversa "Variegata"

Cryptomeria japonica "Globosa Nana"

Elaeagnus angustifolia

Eupatorium purpureum

Euphorbia spp. and cultivars

Hamamelis mollis

Humulus lupulus "Aureus"

Juniperus spp.

Lunaria annua "Alba Variegata"

Nothofagus fusca

Ophiopogon planiscapus "Nigrescens"

Parthenocissus quinquefolia

Phormium tenax Purpureum Group

Picea pungens glauca

Prunus lusitanica

Pyracantha spp. and cultivars

Stachys byzantina

Symphoricarpos albus

Vitis spp. and cultivars

Any soil in shade or semi-shade

Acer spp

Alchemilla mollis

Alnus glutinosa "Imperialis"

Astrantia major "Sunningdale Variegated"

Azara microphylla

Brassica oleracea

Briza maxima

Corylus avellana "Contorta"

Cotoneaster spp.

Hedera colchica "Dentata Variegata"

Hedera colchica "Sulphur Heart"

Ilex spp.

Pinus spp.

Taxus spp.

Vinca major "Variegata"

Any soil in sun

Acer spp.

Actinidia kolomikta

Alchemilla mollis

Alnus glutinosa "Imperialis"

Astrantia major "Sunningdale Variegated"

Azara microphylla

Betula spp.

Brassica oleracea

Briza maxima

Calocedrus decurrens

Catalpa bignonioides "Aurea"

Corylus avellana "Contorta"

Cotoneaster spp.

Elymus magellanicus

Eriobotrya japonica

Fagus sylvatica "Aspleniifolia" and "Rohanii"

Geranium macrorrhizum "Album"

Hedera colchica "Dentata Variegata"

Hedera colchica "Sulphur Heart"

Ilex spp.

Koeleria vallesiana

Koelreuteria paniculata

Lychnis coronaria

Phalaris arundinacea "Picta"

Pinus spp

Prunus spp.

Rheum palmatum "Atrosanguineum"

Robinia pseudoacacia "Frisia"

Rosa rubrifolia

Rubus spp.

Taxus spp.

Vinca major "Variegata"

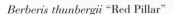
Berberis thunbergii "Red Pillar"

Alchemilla mollis

Astrantia major "Sunningdale Variegated"

Where to see and study foliage plants

Note: Most of the places listed are public botanical gardens or arboreta. They offer ideal situations for studying locally adapted plants valued for leaf, bark, and berry. An outstanding reference for locating plants available in commerce is *Andersen Horticultural Library's Source List of Plants and Seeds*, the latest edition available through the Andersen Horticultural Library, University of Minnesota Libraries, Minnesota Landscape Arboretum, 3675 Arboretum Dr., Chanhassen, MN 55317.

UNITED STATES

American Horticultural Society
River Farm
7931 East Boulevard Dr.
Alexandra, VA 22308

The Arnold Arboretum of
Harvard University
125 Arborway
Jamaica Plain, MA 02130-2795

Atlanta Botanical Garden in
Piedmont Park
P.O. Box 77246
Atlanta, GA 30357

Berkshire Botanical Garden
Stockbridge, MA 01262

The Berry Botanic Garden
11505 SW Summerville Ave.
Portland, OR 97219

Birmingham Botanical Gardens
2612 Lane Park Rd.
Birmingham, AL 35223

The Bloedel Reserve
7571 NE Dolphin Dr.
Bainbridge Island, WA 98110-1097

Botanica, The Wichita Gardens
701 Amidon
Wichita, KS 67203

Brooklyn Botanic Garden
1000 Washington Ave.
Brooklyn, NY 11225

Brookside Gardens
1500 Glenallen Ave.
Wheaton, MD 20902

Callaway Gardens
Highway 27
Pine Mountain, GA 31822

Sedum spectabile "Autumn Joy"

The Central Park Conservatory
Garden
105th St. and Fifth Ave.
Offices at The Arsenal
830 Fifth Ave.
New York, NY 10021

Chicago Botanic Garden
Lake Cook Rd.
Glencoe, IL 60022

Cleveland Botanic Garden
11030 East Blvd.
Cleveland, OH 44106

Dallas Arboretum & Botanical Garden
8617 Garland Rd.
Dallas, TX 75218

Denver Botanic Garden
909 York St.
Denver, CO 80206

Duke Gardens
P.O. Box 2030
Route 206 South
Somerville, NJ 08876

Fairchild Tropical Garden
10901 Old Cutler Rd.
Miami, FL 33156

Filoli
Canada Rd.
Woodside, CA 94062

Fort Worth Botanic Garden
3220 Botanic Garden Dr.
Fort Worth, TX 76107

Foster Botanic Garden
50 North Vineyard Blvd.
Honolulu, Oahu, HI 96817

Ginter, Lewis, Botanical Garden
1800 Lakeside Ave.
P.O. Box 28246
Richmond, VA 23228-4610

Greer Gardens
1280 Goodpasture Island Rd.
Eugene, OR 97401

The Holden Arboretum
9500 Sperry Rd.
Mentor, OH 44060

Huntington Botanical Gardens
1151 Oxford Rd.
San Marino, CA 91108

Innisfree Garden
Millbrook, NY 12545

Longwood Gardens
Kennett Square, PA 19348-0501

Los Angeles State and County
Arboretum
301 North Baldwin Ave.
Arcadia, CA 91006-2697

Harold L. Lyon Arboretum
University of Hawaii at Manoa
3860 Manoa Rd.
Honolulu, Oahu, HI 96822

Meadowbrook Farm
1633 Washington Lane
Meadowbrook, PA 19046

Memphis Botanic Garden
750 Cherry Rd.
Memphis, TN 38117

Mercer Arboretum and Botanical
Garden
22306 Aldine-Westfield Rd.
Humble, TX 77338

Minnesota Landscape Arboretum
3675 Arboretum Dr.
Chanhassen, MN 55317

Morris Arboretum of the University of
Pennsylvania
9414 Meadowbrook Ave.
Philadelphia, PA 19118

Morton Arboretum
Route 53
Lisle, IL 60532

New Orleans Botanical Garden
Victory Ave. City Park
New Orleans, LA 70119

The New York Botanical Garden
Bronx, NY 10458-5126

North Carolina Botanical Garden
UNC-CH Totten Center 457A
Chapel Hill, NC 27514

Old Westbury Gardens
71 Old Westbury Rd.
Old Westbury, NY 11568

Phipps Conservatory
Department of Parks
400 City County Building
Pittsburgh, PA 15219

Planting Fields Arboretum
Planting Fields Rd.
Oyster Bay, NY 11771

Rosa rugosa "Scabrosa"

Virginia Robinson Gardens
1008 Elden Way
Beverly Hills, CA 90210

San Antonio Botanical Gardens
555 Funston Pl.
San Antonio, TX 78209

Santa Barbara Botanic Garden
1212 Mission Canyon Rd.
Santa Barbara, CA 93105

Scott Arboretum
Swarthmore College
Swarthmore, PA 19081

Selby, Marie, Botanical Gardens
811 South Palm Ave.
Sarasota, FL 34236

Strybing Arboretum and Botanical
Gardens
Ninth Ave. at Lincoln Way
San Francisco, CA 94122

U. S. Botanic Garden
245 First St. SW
Washington, D.C. 20024

U. S. National Arboretum
3501 New York Ave. NE
Washington, D.C. 20002

Wave Hill
675 West 252nd St.
Bronx, NY 10471

CANADA

The Butchart Gardens
Benvenuto Rd.
P.O. Box 4010 Sta. A
Victoria, BC V8X 3X4

Montreal Botanical Garden
4101 Sherbrooke St.
Montreal, PQ H1X 2B2

Royal Botanical Gardens
P.O. Box 399
Hamilton, ON L8N 3H8

University of British Columbia
Botanical Garden
6250 Stadium Rd.
Vancouver, BC V6T 1W5

Index

Further Reading

Bloom, Adrian. *Winter Garden Glory*. New York: HarperCollins , 1995.
Chatto, Beth. *The Green Tapestry*. New York: HarperCollins, 1989.
———. *The Dry Garden*. London: Dent, 1988.
Darke, Rick. *Ornamental Grasses*. Boston: Little, Brown & Co., 1994.
Druse, Ken and Margaret Roach. *The Natural Habitat Garden*. New York: Crown Pub. Group, 1994.
Gladdstein, Judy. *Garden Design with Foliage*. Pownal, Vt.: Garden Way Publishing, 1991.
Grenfell, Diana. *The Gardener's Guide to Growing Hostas*. Portland, Oreg.: Timber Press, 1996
Grounds, Roger. *Ferns*. New York: Pelham Books, 1974.
———. *Ornamental Grasses*. North Pomfret, Vt.: Trafalgar Square, 1990.
Hansen, Richard and Friedrich Stahl. *Perennials and Their Garden Habitats*. 4th ed. Translated by Richard Ward. Portland, Oreg.: Timber Press, 1993.
Lacy, Allen. *Gardening with Groundcovers and Vines*. New York: HarperCollins, 1993.
Lloyd, Christopher. *Foliage Plants*. rev. ed. New York: Penguin, 1987.
Mulligan, William C. *Rare and Unusual Plants*. New York: Simon & Schuster, 1993.
McDonald, Elvin. *400 Best Garden Plants*. New York: Random House, 1995.
Rix, Martyn & Roger Phillips. *Shrubs*. New York: Macmillan, 1989.
Thorpe, Patricia. *Growing Pains*. San Francisco: Harcourt Brace, 1994.
Verey, Rosemary. *The Garden in Winter*. Portland, Oreg.: Timber Press, 1989.
Vertrees, J. D. *Japanese Maples*. 2d ed. Portland, Oreg.: Timber Press, 1987.
Yang, Linda. *The City and Town Gardener*. New York: Random House, 1990.

Picture Acknowledgements

Brian Carter/Garden Picture Library 114 (right): David England/Garden Picture Library 115 (right); John Glover/Garden Picture Library 115 (left), 112

Clive Nichols would like to acknowledge the kind cooperation of the designers, organizations, and owners who gave permission to photograph the pictures on the following pages: 7 Preen Manor, Salop., England; 11 Herterton House, Northumberland, England; 12 High Beeches Garden, W. Sussex, England; 13 The Sir Harold Hillier Gardens and Arboretum, Hants., England; 15 Bourton House, Glos., England; 16 Designer Olivia Clark; 17 Designer Jill Billington; 18 Hatfield House, Herts., England; 19 Wollerton Old Hall, Salop., England; 20 Designer Olivia Clark; 21 (left) La Casella, France (right) The Huntington Botanical Gardens; 23 Harcourt Arboretum, Oxon., England; 26 City of Bath Botanical Gardens, England; 27 Ling Beeches,Yorks., England; 28 (left) Designer Sheila Jackson, London (right) Designer Sharon Osmond, San Francisco; 29 Herterton House, Northumberland, England; 32 Winkworth Arboretum, Surrey, England; 34 (below left) Ling Beeches, Yorks., England; 35 (below left) Ling Beeches, Yorks., England (right) Spinners, Hants., England; 36 The Royal Horticultural Society's Garden, Wisley, Surrey, England; 37 The Manor House, Walton-in-Gordano, Bristol, England; 38 (left) Chenies Manor House, Bucks., England (right) Designer Olivia Clark; 40 (left) Longacre, Kent, England; 41 Designer Rupert Golby; 42 The Herb Farm, Sonning, Berks., England; 44 Ling Beeches, Yorks., England; 49 The Dingle, Welshpool, Wales; 51 The Valley Gardens, Surrey, England; 52-55 Wollerton Old Hall, Salop., England; 61 The Old Rectory, Sudborough, Northants., England; 66-69 Hadspen House Garden and Nursery, Designers Sandra and Nori Pope; 77 Lower House Farm, Gwent, Wales; 79 The Dingle, Welshpool, Wales.

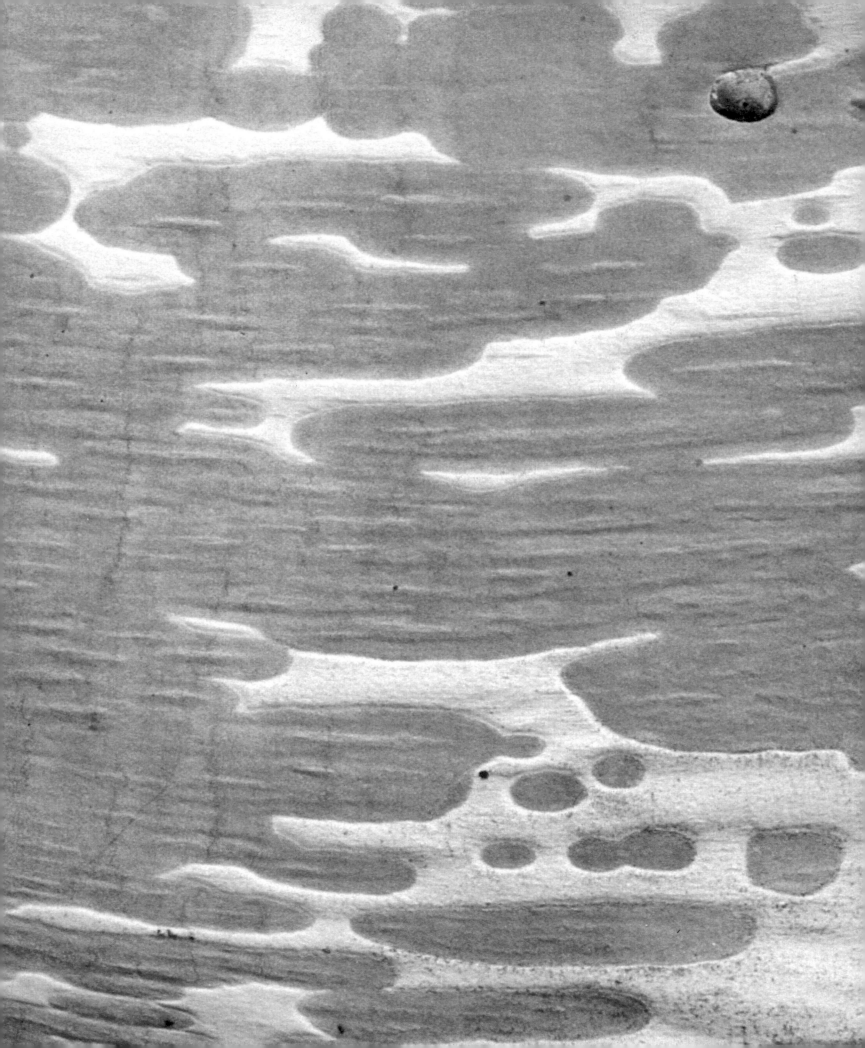